SALMON

SALMON

An Angler's Guide

TIMOTHY FREW

MALLARD
PRESS

MALLARD PRESS
An imprint of BDD Promotional Book Company, Inc.
666 Fifth Avenue
New York, New York 10103

A FRIEDMAN GROUP BOOK

Published by MALLARD PRESS
An imprint of BDD Promotional Book Company, Inc.
666 Fifth Avenue
New York, New York 10103

Mallard Press and its accompanying design and logo are
trademarks of BDD Promotional Book Company, Inc.

First published in the United States of America in 1991
by The Mallard Press.

ISBN 0-792-45293-3

SALMON: An Angler's Guide
was prepared and produced by
Michael Friedman Publishing Group, Inc.
15 West 26th Street
New York, New York 10010

Editor: Sharyn Rosart
Art Director: Jeff Batzli
Designer: Susan Livingston
Photo Researcher: Daniella Jo Nilva

Typeset by EAC/Interface
Color separations by Universal Colour Scanning Ltd.
Printed and bound in Hong Kong by Leefung-Asco Printers Ltd.

DEDICATION

To my nephew, Harry Zittel, and my future niece or nephew, who will probably be born just about the same time this book is released.

ACKNOWLEDGMENTS

Thank you to my editor, Sharyn Rosart, for always finding something funny about fish; the designer, Sue Livingston, for having the patience to deal with me on three fishing books; and to Marc Sapir and Karen Greenberg, the production team, because they got such a kick out of the fact that I acknowledged them on my first book.

TABLE OF CONTENTS

INTRODUCTION

The salmon has long been revered as one of the world's premiere freshwater game fish. Its long, sturdy body and driven nature make it a worthy adversary for even the most experienced anglers. Ichthyologists

From top to bottom: *Pink salmon, coho salmon, steelhead trout, and another coho salmon.* Opposite page: *A group of anglers float down the Kenai River in Alaska while fishing for salmon.*

have devoted endless hours and resources to the study of this remarkable fish, yet still they know very little about its nature and behavior. Why do salmon return to their native streams, like clockwork, year after year, to spawn? What drives them to give up eating and make the life-or-death drive upstream to the waters in which they were born? Why do Pacific salmon die immediately after spawning, while their Atlantic cousins may survive to spawn three or four consecutive years? Why do migrating Atlantic salmon meet up with European Atlantic salmon off the coast of Greenland while on their yearly oceanic journey? The more scientists study these mysterious fish, the more questions arise.

For the angler, the salmon represents the ultimate fishing challenge. In eastern Canada, anglers gladly spend thousands of dollars every year for the chance to catch just a few of these elusive fish. On the West Coast, scores of party boats troll the rough ocean waters every day in hopes of finding a hungry school of Chinook or

© Alissa Crandall

coho salmon. It is important to understand the behavior, the habitat, and the feeding characteristics of your quarry. If you use the wrong type of fly or fish in the wrong parts of the stream when hunting down the Atlantic salmon, you may be in for a very frustrating and expensive fishing trip. There are several types of salmon available to the angler and each type behaves according to its own set of rules, which are determined both by genetic makeup and the peculiarities of the aquatic environment. As a result, there are different techniques employed for each

type of fish. For example, it is against the law to fish for Atlantic salmon in North America with anything but fly tackle. Also, because they don't feed while spawning, the angler must try to tease or anger the fish into striking. On the other hand, with landlocked salmon, the angler is able to use a wide variety of baits and lures and can fish for them at times other than the spawning season.

This book takes a look at the appearance, habitat, range, spawning habits, feeding characteristics, and migratory trends of the major salmon varieties. In addition, it

provides pointers on equipment, angling techniques, and the best places and times of year to angle for each fish. This book does, however, come with a warning: Nothing written here should be regarded as the ultimate angling truth. Any angler worth his or her salt knows that there are no real rules to fishing. What works one day may be completely worthless the next. What remains true, however, is that by learning as much about fish as possible, and by clocking many hours on the stream, any angler can improve his or her technique and luck.

Chapter 1

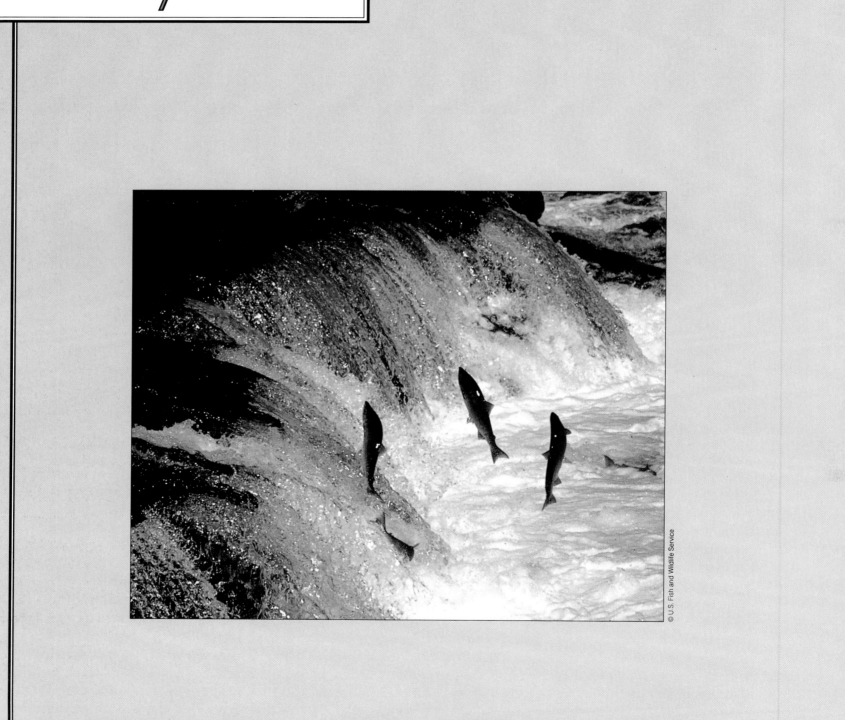

THE CIRCLE OF LIFE

The spawning run of the salmon is one of the most spectacular sights in nature. Driven by an age-old instinct, scores of these determined fish leave their oceanic feeding grounds and make a desperate rush

© Thomas D. Mangelsen/Images of Nature

Left: *Few sights are more spectacular than salmon making a charge upstream to their spawning grounds.* **Right:** *One-month-old chums are extremely vulnerable to predators.*

upstream to their place of birth. They forgo eating and rest only periodically as they fight swift currents, manmade obstacles, and hungry predators. Confronted by a waterfall or pounding rapids, salmon will make mad dashes and hurl themselves through the air—sometimes as high as 7 feet (2 m). They will jump again and again, flaying themselves on rocks and logs, until they either clear the obstacle or die trying.

The spawning run is the climax of a life that began as a tiny, fertilized pink egg in a gravel redd, or nest at the bottom of a cold, swift-running stream. The eggs are laid in the female-built redd and simultaneously fertilized by the male. Once all the eggs are deposited—up to two thousand in a single redd—the female covers the nest with a layer of fine gravel. There the eggs incubate for anywhere from fifty to one hundred days, depending on the water temperature.

The parents, however, never see the product of their struggles. Pacific salmon always die soon after spawning. A few Atlantic salmon survive the spawning run, but are well on

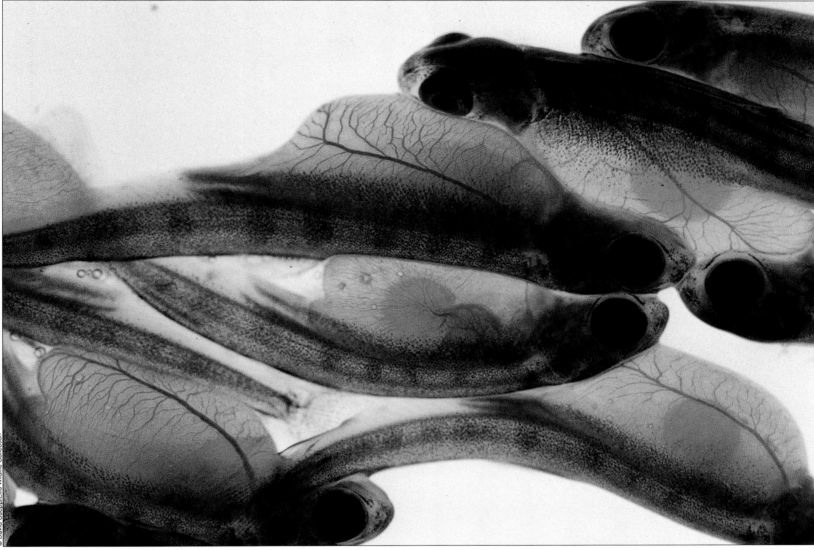

© David Csepp/Ellis Wildlife Collection

their way back to the ocean by the time the eggs hatch.

Salmon begin life as tiny, translucent alevins. They have spotted backs, black eyes, and small yolk sacs attached to their bellies. The alevins remain in the redd for several weeks until they reach a length of about 1 inch (2.5 cm), and until their yolk sac is exhausted. Once they emerge from the gravelly bottom they are referred to as fry. These tiny fish immediately begin foraging for food, feeding mostly on the plankton, insect larvae, and nymphs that cling to the underwater rocks. Fry are sensitive to light and hide in deep water, under stones or in shaded areas, during the day. After dusk, they move into shallower areas to feed.

Life as a salmon fry is precarious. These extremely vulnerable fish are a favorite food staple of a wide variety of predators, including larger salmon, Dolly Varden char, squawfish, cutthroat trout, sculpins, water birds, snakes, and others. In fact, the vast majority of salmon never make it past their first year. In *The Salmon: Their Fight for Survival*, author Anthony Netboy cites a study by noted sockeye salmon expert Dr. R. E. Foerster, who estimates that out of 2 million fertilized eggs, only 950,000 fry will be produced, out of which a mere 19,000 will reach the sea.

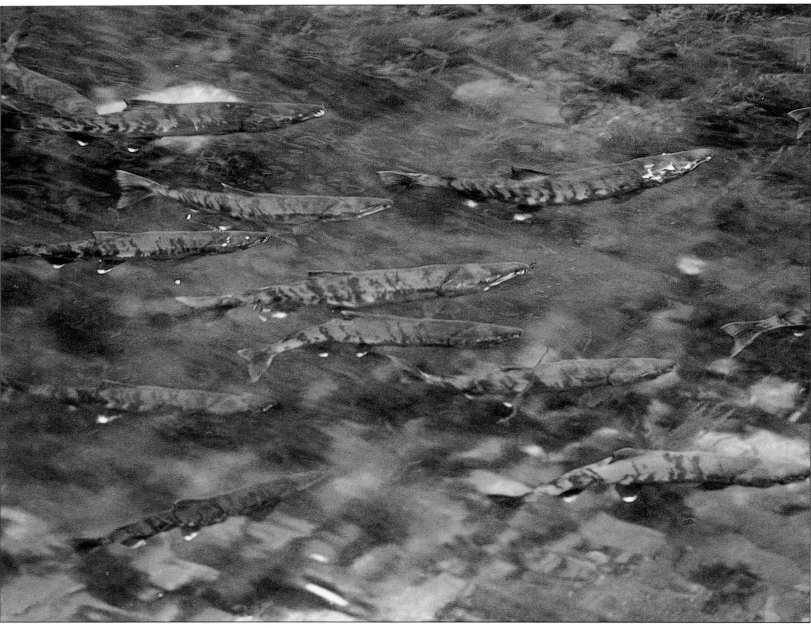

© David Csepp/Ellis Wildlife Collection

Aside from natural predators, juvenile salmon also have to withstand myriad human-caused threats. The encroachment of civilization, rising pollution levels, and the building of hydroelectric dams have all contributed to the declining salmon populations. Netboy states that the creation of reservoirs on the Columbia River by hydroelectric dams has led to "an explosion of squawfish and other predator fish, [which have] become a major menace to juvenile salmon."

Once salmon fry reach about 2 inches (5 cm) they are referred to as parr or fingerlings. (Atlantic salmon at this stage are usually called parr, while Pacific salmon are called fingerlings.) They develop brown backs, silvery bellies, and black and red spots running down their backs and lateral lines. In addition, all Atlantic salmon and most Pacific salmon develop a series of highly visible dark

© Clyde H. Smith/FPG International

stripes, or parr marks, down each side. Pinks and chum, two species of Pacific salmon, usually migrate to sea as fry and thus develop only faint parr marks.

It is during the parr or fingerling stage that salmon do most of their early growing. During the summer months, when insect hatches abound, these young salmon feed voraciously and begin to acquire the size, strength, and swimming ability they need in their future life in the ocean. The amount of time young salmon remain in fresh water varies from species to species. As stated earlier, pink and chum salmon migrate to sea almost immediately after reaching the fry stage, whereas most other strains of Pacific salmon stay in fresh water for one to two years. Atlantic salmon, on the other hand, usually stay in fresh water much longer. In relatively warm regions, such as Maine and southern Canada, they migrate after two years, while in the subarctic regions of Iceland and Greenland, they may remain in fresh water for four to five years.

Just prior to their downstream journey to the ocean, juvenile salmon go through a series of dramatic physiological changes, known as smoltification. Their tails become longer and more deeply forked, their parr marks disappear, their bodies become more muscular and develop a silvery hue. After about two months, instinct drives these smolts out of their natal waters and into the sea. In most areas, this oceanward migration takes place in April or May, just after the spring rains have raised water levels enough to aid their journey.

Unlike the spawning-age salmon, which travel mostly during the day, these ocean-bound smolts migrate

A school of Chinook parr make their way to the ocean. Note the dark parr marks running up and down their sides.

Life Stages of the Salmon

Alevin	Newly hatched, translucent salmon with yolk sac. Less than 1 inch (2.5 cm) long.
Fry	One- to two-inch (2.5- to 5-cm) long salmon that have depleted their yolk sacs and emerged from the redd.
Parr or Fingerlings	Young salmon with visible markings known as parr marks. Feed voraciously on insects and small freshwater crustaceans.
Smolt	Young salmon that have undergone physiological changes and are ready to go to sea.
Grilse	Atlantic salmon that spend only one year at sea before returning to spawn.
Salmon	Mature stage of the fish that returns to the river to spawn.
Kelt	Atlantic salmon (or steelhead trout) that have spawned, and are enroute back to the ocean.

only at night. On some short rivers and streams the smolts are able to make the entire journey in one night, while in longer rivers they must stop and rest during the day behind large rocks or in deep pools or riffles. Although it's not quite as treacherous as the upstream run, many smolts nevertheless perish during the trek downstream. They fall prey to predators, get smashed against rocks and logs when traversing cascading waterfalls or high dams, or get hopelessly lost in irrigation canals and ditches that divert them from their course. It is estimated that only about 30 percent of all smolts make it all the way to the ocean.

Once they reach salt water, the smolts remain in the bays and saltwater estuaries for a period of time ranging from several weeks to a few months, acclimating themselves to their new saline environment. They feed voraciously during this time and grow rapidly. Their diet consists primarily of tiny saltwater shrimp, which gives salmon their distinctive, pink-colored flesh. (Many wild trout that feed on tiny freshwater shrimp

also have pink flesh.) Salmon are extremely vulnerable during their transition to saltwater. They must learn to eat new foods, recognize and avoid new predators, and traverse unfamiliar waters. Birds, seals, and bears often line the banks of saltwater estuaries and feast on the young salmon. Once in the ocean, these fish remain vulnerable because they are a favorite quarry of larger predators such as tuna, swordfish, pollock, and killer whales.

Opposite page: *A mature Chinook* (left) *and pink salmon* (right) *begin their journey back to their spawning streams.* Right: *Many running salmon fall victim to predators such as this bear.*

© Gary Crandall/Envision

As they grow, salmon develop strong jaws, sharp teeth, and hard scales. These physiological changes provide them with protection and help them compete for food in the difficult ocean environment. Soon their diet shifts to small fish such as anchovies, pilchards, and herring in addition to shrimp and squid.

As soon as the salmon sufficiently adjust themselves to ocean life, they begin a migration that may take them thousands of miles from their natal streams. Most strains of Pacific salmon follow the currents north toward the Bering Sea and Alaska, traveling at the rate of 15 miles (24 km) a day for months on end. They then turn south and swim deep into the Pacific Ocean, eventually heading back toward their place of origin. Depending on how long they remain at sea before returning to spawn, Pacific salmon may repeat this 2,000-mile (3200-km) elliptical journey several times. It is estimated that many salmon travel more than 10,000 miles (16,000 km) in the ocean before returning to their home rivers to spawn. While different

Onlookers admire a school of sockeye salmon running upstream at the Kenai Peninsula, Alaska.

strains of Pacific salmon have slightly different migration patterns, almost all of them will travel in a counterclockwise, circular, or elliptical pattern that roughly follows the oceanic currents.

The voyage of the Atlantic salmon differs drastically from that of the Pacific. Instead of traveling in an elliptical pattern, Atlantic salmon immediately head northeast for the rich feeding waters around Greenland, where they may remain for several years, until it is time to return to spawn. Here, North American salmon meet up with their European cousins, in what could be described as an Atlantic Salmon League of Nations. Tagging experiments have recorded salmon from as far away as the Gulf of Bothnia (3,000 miles [4800 km] away) on the west coast of Greenland. Atlantic salmon remain in the ocean from one to five years before returning home to spawn.

Life in the ocean takes a heavy toll. Only about 10 percent of those salmon that go to sea eventually make it back to the river to spawn. Scientists know very little about what

Also known as the humpback, mature pink salmon develop a pronounced bulge just behind their head.

drives the salmon to return to its native stream. What is known is that these fish make their spawning runs with uncanny regularity. Yet not all salmon of the same species and from the same river follow the same timetable. Although all salmon spawn in the fall, their actual run upstream is staggered from early spring to fall. Some salmon reach their spawning grounds months before spawning actually takes place.

When they reach the mouth of their spawning stream, salmon congregate and rest until they are reacclimated to fresh water. Once again their bodies undergo dramatic changes. Their skin thickens, their scales are absorbed and their bodies become more compressed. Male salmon develop a hooked jaw, while females begin to produce roe. In addition, each species regains its own distinctive freshwater markings. Atlantic salmon turn to a coppery pink color, the sockeye turns bright red with a pale green head, and the male of the pink salmon grows a large hump.

They remain at the mouth of their stream, awaiting the heavy rains that will raise the water levels high enough for them to begin their journey. It seems as if a salmon's entire life is devoted to preparing for this moment: While at sea they grow strong and become adept swimmers. A few months before their return to fresh water, they step up their already ravenous feeding in order to store up the fats and oils they will need to sustain them on their upstream journey.

Bears, birds, humans, and other predators begin lining the banks of the rivers, waiting for the salmon run

© Chris Huss/Ellis Wildlife Collection

A sockeye salmon makes one final lunge over some rapids (left), as a school of kokenee salmon briefly rests before continuing their journey upstream.

Some Pacific salmon make upstream journeys of 1,000 miles (1600 km) or more, traveling at a rate of 50 to 100 miles (80 to 160 km) a day. This is no small feat considering that most of these northwestern rivers are full of swift moving rapids and cascading falls. In addition, salmon do not eat while on their spawning run. Instead they live off the oils and fats they stored up while in the ocean.

By the time they reach their spawning waters, they are battered, cut, exhausted, and laden with roe and milt, yet they still have work to do. The salmon pair off to mate. Then the female faces upstream, turns on her side, and begins scooping out gravel with her tail while the male fights off any other suitors. The female continues digging until the redd, or nest, is deep enough to protect her precious eggs from the strong current of the river. The finished redd measures up to 2 feet (60 cm) long and between 6 inches (15 cm) and 1 foot (30 cm) deep.

Just prior to mating, a brief courtship dance takes place. The female rests in the bottom of her redd while

to begin. Then, finally, the rains come, raising the rivers and oxygenating the water and the first salmon begin their fervent rush upstream.

Traveling only by day, they take the upstream run in a series of starts and stops. The fish traverse a set of rapids or leap over a waterfall and then find a calm pool or riffle in which to rest. Salmon are very adept at finding spots where they can stop and regain

their energy. Even in swift-moving water, they rest behind rocks that cut the current, or they locate the edges of a current, where they need a minimal amount of strength to maintain their position. Salmon do most of their swimming in the early morning or evening, when the light is dim. During mid-afternoon they usually rest in the cool shade of an undercut bank or overhanging tree.

Adult male and female coho salmon prepare to spawn. Note their pronounced spawning colors and their hooked upper jaws.

© Chris Huss/Ellis Wildlife Collection

the male swims back and forth above, occasionally nudging her with his nose or caressing her with his fins. Eventually he moves his body over hers and they simultaneously release eggs and milt into the redd. While most salmon spawn one-on-one, other mating patterns—usually several males to one female—are not uncommon. Because spawning usually takes place in relatively strong currents, the cloudy milt may be washed downstream before the eggs are fertilized. When more than one male spawns with a single female, the chances of fertilization increase.

Once the eggs are deposited in the redd and fertilized, the female moves slightly upstream and begins covering the nest with gravel. This top layer of gravel helps protect the eggs from the current and from hungry predators, while allowing enough oxygen to reach the eggs so that incubation can take place.

A few days after spawning, the Pacific salmon die. Many Atlantic salmon, on the other hand, survive the ordeal and remain in the stream or river until they regain enough

The life cycle of the salmon has been developing since the fish's ancestors first appeared more than 135 million years ago. The species has survived through glacial movements, changing climates, and continental shifts; however, today the fish's existence is threatened by pollution, river development, and commercial overfishing.

strength to return to the ocean. These surviving salmon are called kelts, or black salmon. They stay in fresh water throughout the winter by lowering their metabolism and return to the ocean in the spring. Some Atlantic salmon survive long enough to spawn up to four times.

The salmon's life cycle, as arduous as it may seem, has been developing and changing since the fish's ancestors first appeared more than 135 million years ago. Scientists are not in agreement as to whether the salmon was originally a freshwater or a saltwater fish. The species has, however, survived through many fluctuations in its natural habitats. Glacial movements, continental shifts, and changing climates have all altered the day to day life of the salmon. Yet, through it all the fish has survived. Today, the salmon's greatest menace comes from the earth's human population. Unless mankind takes steps to halt or reverse the current threats of pollution, river development, and commercial overfishing, the future of these magnificent fish will grow increasingly dim.

© Bob Peterson/FPG International

EQUIPMENT FOR THE SALMON ANGLER

The salmon is an extremely strong, agile fish. Once hooked, it will leap from the water, make long, rod-bending runs, and attempt to snag or break your line on some sort of obstruction. Equipment is of the

utmost importance in battling this venerable opponent. The rods, reels, and lines used in salmon fishing must be able to take a lot of punishment, so make a point of purchasing a quality outfit. No matter how experienced an angler you are you simply cannot catch many fish with faulty equipment.

As with all types of fishing, the specific equipment you use depends on individual angling situations. Surf casting for Pacific salmon requires different equipment than trolling for landlockeds. In the case of Atlantic salmon, the law requires that you use fly tackle, but even within this category there is a wide variety to choose from. Following is a brief overview of the types of equipment used in fishing for salmon. Throughout the book are more detailed descriptions of the most popular outfits for particular situations.

FLY FISHING

Surely, the graceful, yet accurate, cast of the fly angler must be one of the most beautiful sights to be seen in all of angling. The line arches gently through the air as the angler skillfully moves the rod to and fro, gaining momentum. Finally, one last long backswing. Just as the line plays out completely behind the angler, he or she brings it forward into a perfect rolling cast.

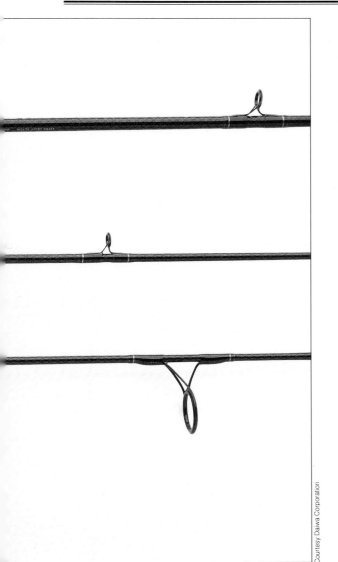

Courtesy Daiwa Corporation

In North America, it is illegal to fish for Atlantic salmon using anything but fly equipment. Spinning and bait-casting equipment can, however, be used for catching Pacific salmon.

© Louis Borie/Photo/Nats

A solitary fly angler drifts his line on Long Lake in Colorado.

It is the simple, elegant motion of the fly cast that attracts many anglers to fly fishing. It is also one of the most important aspects to fishing for Atlantic salmon. These large spawning fish do not eat while they are in fresh water, so they must be angered or teased into striking. The casting and proper presentation of the salmon fly is crucial to success. It takes many, many years for the expert salmon angler to hone his craft, and even the greatest anglers of all time come up empty-handed on the Miramichi every now and then.

Many experienced bait casters are so intimidated by the complexity of catching salmon or trout on a fly that they never even attempt it. This is a shame; for despite the mystique surrounding the sport, fly fishing is really based on just a few simple techniques and concepts. Once these basics are learned, the angler can go forth and enthusiastically pursue this sport, always striving to improve. And that is the challenge that keeps fly fishermen coming back: The technique can always be improved upon, but it can never really be perfected.

Because the casting and proper presentation of the fly is so important in this type of fishing, appropriate equipment is crucial to success. The next few pages serve as a primer to the different components that make up a fly-fishing outfit. If you are a newcomer who is just becoming interested in fly fishing, I would heartily recommend you read a few of the many excellent books on fly fishing, including *Fly Fishing: A Beginner's Guide* by David Lee and *Trout on a Fly* by Lee Wulff.

The rod is arguably the single most important piece of equipment in the fly angler's repertoire. It is through the action of this device that the angler delivers the fly to its destination. If you have a poor-quality rod or one unsuited to your particular angling situation, you will most likely not be able to cast accurately... and if you can't bring the fly to the fish, you can't catch the fish.

Salmon rods have a much-vaunted history. For hundreds of years, the traditional salmon rod was a cumbersome 12- to 15-foot (3.6- to 4.5-m) fly rod weighing as much as 30 ounces (840 g). Two hands were used for casting, and, while these rods could cast long distances, accuracy and touch were often sacrificed. Although a few of these monster rods are still used in parts of Europe, today the trend is toward lighter, single-handed rods that are sometimes not much longer than those used for trout.

Fly fishing is different from spin casting or bait casting in that instead of casting the lure or bait, you are actually casting the line, which pulls the fly along with it. It is the weight of the line that bends, or loads, the fly rod on the backcast, then as you bring the rod forward the rod springs back, propelling the line and the fly to their destination.

Courtesy G-Loomis, inset photo: © Jonathan Swain

A well-crafted fly rod is a thing of beauty to the devoted angler. Left: The Gary Loomis 9-foot (3-m) fly rod. Below: The Des Chutes 9-foot (3-m) western rod.

Rod Materials

The composition of the fly rod has changed drastically over the past 150 years. Originally all rods were made of solid wood, and subsequently of the flexible, yet strong, bamboo cane. Over the past century, modern technology has provided the fly angler with a variety of choices when buying a rod. Of course, the bamboo rod still exists, and quite often is cherished as a well-made piece of equipment and valued heirloom; but now it is joined by rods made of fiberglass and graphite.

• **Bamboo** The bamboo fly rod is one of the most carefully constructed and responsive artifacts available to the fly angler. Even though some graphite and fiberglass rods have equaled, or even surpassed, bamboo in overall performance, none can come even close to matching its grace, beauty, and what many traditionalists refer to as its feel. Because of the craftsmanship involved in their construction, bamboo rods are very expensive. They can range in price from six hundred to several thousand dollars. While this price tag may seem prohibitive to most anglers, a bamboo rod can be looked upon as an investment, for it will continue to perform well year after year and even generation after generation.

• **Fiberglass** Fiberglass was the first material to post a challenge to the bamboo rod industry. When fiberglass rods came on the scene after the 1940s, they were the lightest, strongest, most affordable rods available.

Today, however, the bamboo rod is still going strong, and the fiberglass rod is most threatened by the development of graphite. While it is relatively lightweight, fiberglass is still heavier than graphite, and graphite rods offer more power and higher sensitivity at a comparable price.

• **Graphite** Graphite is a product of the carbon-fiber technology developed by the modern aerospace

Courtesy Orvis Company, Inc.

industry. It is a resilient, lightweight fiber that has a "high modulus of elasticity," which means more snap for the fly angler. Graphite rods have only been around since 1973; however, they have quickly taken the fishing industry by storm. They combine light weight, high power, and a good feel in a rod that will perform well in virtually any fishing situation. While high-quality graphite rods are generally more expensive than glass rods, their added perform-

ance more than makes up for the price difference.

Rod Length

The length of your fly rod will depend on a number of different factors: the size and type of fish you are catching, the size of the river you are fishing, and your personal preference. As stated earlier, the salmon fly rod was traditionally a very long and cumbersome piece of equipment. As the sport has developed, however,

rods have gradually gotten shorter and lighter. Still, the size and strength of the salmon require a heavier line and, often, a longer rod than is required for trout fishing. Of course, expert salmon anglers are constantly trying to push the limits of rod length in order to test their abilities. Many will use the lightest line and the shortest rod possible to get the job done, putting more emphasis on their angling ability than the strength of their equipment.

Left: *An angler battles a trout with a graphite fly rod on the Baptism River in Tettegouche State Park, Minnesota.* Right: *A well-balanced fly outfit is crucial to angling success.*

The size of your rod will also depend to a degree upon the conditions you are fishing in. Most anglers use either an 8½-foot (2.5-m), for normal fishing situations, or a 9- to 9½-foot (2.7- to 2.9-m) rod for casting long distances or into heavy winds. Whatever length rod you choose, it should have a fairly strong backbone and at least moderate casting power.

Line Weight

The weight of your line must be matched to your rod and will depend largely on what type of situations you will be fishing in. The chart below serves as a rough guide to help you match your line weight to your fishing situation. The weight numbers, 1 through 12, were developed by the American Fishing Tackle Manufacturers Association (AFTMA). They correspond to the weight in grains of the first 30 feet (9 m) of line. For example, a 5-weight line weighs 140 grains and a 10-weight weighs 280 grains. The actual weight in grains is not important, but the corresponding AFTMA number is.

Line Weight

Line Weight	Fishing Situation
2 to 4	The lightest fly lines available, these weights are for the experienced fly angler who is fishing for small, easily frightened browns and brookies in narrow clear streams. They create a minimum of disturbance, but are difficult to cast. These lines are not strong enough for pulling in large, strong salmon.
4 to 6	The best line weight for a variety of trout-fishing situations; however, still a bit light for Atlantic and Pacific salmon. Good for casting virtually any type of fly, from small, dry flies and nymphs to long, hairy streamers and bucktails.
6 to 8	These heavy lines are designed for catching big fish in wide fast-flowing rivers and deep lakes, any situation where long, powerful casts are required. Probably the most versatile choice for a wide variety of salmon-fishing situations. Also good for lake trout and steelhead.
8 to 10	These heavier lines require a stiff fly rod for effective casting. The heavyweight line is used primarily for saltwater fly fishing or for big steelhead and salmon.

© Ruth Fairall

© Sally A. Beyer/Positive Reflections

Whether the taper of your fly line is level, double tapered, weighted forward, or shooting will greatly affect the distance and accuracy of your casting.

Line Taper

The taper of a fly line helps control both the accuracy and distance of the cast. There are several different configurations to choose from, each with its own set of casting characteristics.

The most basic and inexpensive type of fly line is the *level line.* This line has the same diameter from one end to the other. As a result, it provides the angler with the least delicacy and casting accuracy.

The *double taper line* is essentially two fly lines in one. It has the same fine taper at each end of the line, which means when one end becomes worn, the angler can simply reverse the line and use the other end. The tapered end makes for smooth, accurate casting and a soft presentation of the line. The double taper is the most popular and expensive of all fly lines.

In recent years, the *weight-forward line* has become increasingly popular among anglers who need to put extra distance in their casts, which is often important in salmon fishing. This fly line concentrates most of its weight up front, in the first

Sinking fly line, such as this made by Orvis, is good for fishing lakes or extremely strong, deep rivers.

Courtesy Orvis Company Inc.

30 feet (9 m) of line, tapering off to a thinner diameter at the middle and back sections. While these lines do allow the angler to cast long and hard, they also sacrifice some accuracy and delicacy of presentation.

For anglers who require even longer casts, such as those fishing for salmon in large, fast-flowing rivers, the *shooting taper,* or *shooting head,* line may be the configuration of choice. Similar to the weight-forward taper, the shooting taper has a weighted front section; however, the taper is then attached to a small diameter running line instead of the larger diameter fly line. Since virtually all of the weight on this line is up front, the angler can release some amazingly long, quick casts.

Line Density

The density of the fly line refers to whether the line sinks, floats, or does both. Most experts recommend that the novice use *floating line.* This is the basic line for fly fishing. While its primary use is for shallow, wet flies and a few dry flies, it can also be used successfully for fishing streamers and nymphs in moderately swift and deep water. Because the line floats on top of the water, it allows the angler to see the fish strike the fly.

The oldest type of fly line is the *sinking line.* As its name states, this line sinks from one end to the other. Today, the angler can select a sinking line according to how fast or deep he or she would like it to sink. In general, these lines are used for fishing deep lakes or extremely strong, deep rivers where the fish are feeding on the bottom.

The *intermediate line* attempts to provide the best qualities of both sinking and floating line. It is an extremely versatile line that uniformly sinks just a few inches below the surface. This line is easy to cast, because of its harder finish, but it's harder to control, because the line is underwater.

One step up from the intermediate line is the *floating-sinking line.* This is essentially a floating fly line with a sinking tip. It allows the angler to fish below the surface, with the added advantage of being able to see the line. Floating-sinking lines come in a variety of configurations: 10-foot (3-m) sinking tips, 20-foot (6-m) sinking tips, and 30-foot (9-m) sinking tips.

Courtesy Orvis Company, Inc.

FLY REELS

The fly reel is probably the least important piece of equipment in the fly angler's arsenal. Its primary function is to store line. It is never used for casting and is seldom used to help haul the fish in. Instead, the fly angler uses his or her hands to strip line in and out when casting or playing a fish. That is not to say, however, that you should cut corners and buy a cheap reel when purchasing a fly outfit. Poorly made reels always break—this can be extremely frustrating, particularly when you've just hooked a hard-fighting fish that is making a desperate run for freedom.

There are several factors to keep in mind when looking for the correct fly reel for your outfit. The first is reel capacity, the amount of fly line and backing line—the braided line wound on the reel and tied to the fly line—that the reel can hold. A quality reel will hold between 50 and 75 yards (45 and 67 m) of backing line in addition to the proper amount of fly line. The amount of actual fly line a reel will hold will depend on the weight of the line. For salmon, the angler may need a reel that can hold between 150 and 160 yards (135 and 144 m) of 8-weight line. Saltwater fly-anglers and anglers

When going after large Atlantic salmon, the angler should have a high-quality fly reel that can hold between 300 and 350 yards (270 and 315 m) of 9 to 11 weight line.

© Sally A. Beyer/Positive Reflections

going after extremely large Atlantic salmon should have reels large enough to hold about 300 to 350 yards (270 to 315 m) of 9- to 11-weight line.

Weight is another important consideration when purchasing a fly reel. The weight of your reel should be matched with the weight of your rod so that the entire outfit is properly balanced. A poorly balanced outfit will make accurate casting very difficult. Salmon rods generally weigh between 9 and 12 ounces (252 and 336 g). The exact weight of the reel will depend on the size of the rod. Talk to fishing shop owners to ensure that you get a properly balanced outfit.

The drag system is the mechanical device that puts friction on the reel as a fish is pulling off line. Most fly reels have a knob-adjusted drag system, which uses triangular-shaped pawls to create friction. As the knob turns, the spring-loaded drag system will put more pressure on the pawls, thereby creating more drag on the line. A quality reel will have two or three pawls, which make them reliable and easy to adjust, while most cheaper reels only have one.

Clockwise from upper left: Rusty Rat, Buck Bug, Salmon Muddler Double, Cosseboom, and Silver Rat are all proven patterns for catching salmon.

FLIES

There are hundreds upon hundreds of fly patterns readily available to the angler. Sporting such unusual names as Pale Evening Dun, Black Bomber, and Woolly Worm, the vast array of these colorful, feathery flies can easily boggle the mind of the novice angler.

Flies are divided into different categories according to what organism they are designed to imitate or suggest and how they are fished. Dry flies are created to closely imitate hatching aquatic insects and are fished on the surface. Wet flies imitate or suggest a variety of subaquatic insects or minnows and are usually fished just below the surface. Streamers, or bucktails, imitate minnows or small fish. Terrestrials suggest land insects that fall or are blown into the water, such as grasshoppers or ants. And finally nymphs imitate the larval forms of aquatic insects.

Because salmon don't eat while on their spawning run, most salmon flies are designed to tease or annoy the fish into striking. With this in mind, the traditional salmon wet flies were designed in gaudy, colorful patterns that would gain the attention of even the most undiscerning fish. Many anglers still swear by these patterns (some as much as a hundred years old) whose names are almost as colorful as the wet flies themselves: Jock Scott, Rusty Rat, Durham Ranger, Lady Amherst, Ratfaced McDougall, Pink Lady, Dusty Miller, Green Highlander, Mar Lodge, and Silver Doctor.

Today, however, more and more anglers are replacing the traditional gaudy patterns with more subdued and simpler hairwig flies—these are

Because salmon are extremely tough fighters that do not tire easily, it is important to put together a strong, high-quality outfit. Cheap equipment will break and may cause you to lose a beauty, such as this freshly netted Pacific salmon (below).

often tied with animal hair instead of feathers. Some of the more modern flies include Cigar Butt, Green Machine, Silver Cosseboom, Butterfly, Hathaway Special, Muddler Minnow, and Black Bomber. The size of the fly depends largely on the conditions of the stream. Most anglers use larger flies (sizes 2 to 4) in the spring when the water is fast and high, and then smaller flies (sizes 6 to 10) later in the season when the water is low and clear.

Salmon will occasionally rise to the dry fly, particularly late in the summer when insects abound. A few proven salmon dry fly patterns include Wilkinson, Whisker, Grey

Heavy-duty bait-casting equipment such as this is ideal for pulling monster Chinook out of the ocean.

Wulff, Irresistible, Mackintosh, and Ratfaced MacDougall.

There is no surefire method for determining exactly what fly to use on what stream in what situation. The seemingly simple act of choosing a fly is a veritable art form. The best advice is to start with a wide variety of proven fly patterns and sizes, ask the advice of anglers who are familiar with a particular stream, and, finally, experiment.

SPINNING AND BAIT-CASTING TACKLE FOR THE PACIFIC SALMON

The law requires that you use fly tackle for the Atlantic salmon in North America; however, when angling for Pacific salmon there are no such restrictions. Since most fishing for Pacific salmon takes place on the ocean, heavy spinning and bait-casting tackle is almost a must. A few anglers do use heavy saltwater fly tackle for pulling in oceangoing salmon; however, this is pretty much limited to when the fish are feeding near the surface or when they are close to shore.

Downriggers allow the angler to troll in deep water while still using relatively light tackle.

The exact type and weight of saltwater tackle you use will depend largely on the style of fishing you are doing at the moment. Most party boats are fitted with short, stiff, heavy-duty trolling rods loaded with wire lines. If you have the aid of a downrigger, lighter tackle can be used. Shore casting for salmon may require a two-handed, 10- to 12-foot (3- to 3.6-m) surf-casting rod with a heavy-duty spinning reel loaded with 250 yards (225 m) of 20-pound (9-kg) test. When casting from a boat, a shorter bait-casting or spinning outfit will do.

Whether you choose spinning or bait-casting equipment is largely a matter of preference. Certain situations may indicate one type of reel over another; however, to a certain degree the two are interchangeable. Throughout the book, I explore the different outfits that are best suited to particular angling situations. For more information on the wide array of equipment available and its uses, I suggest you read one of the many fine books dedicated to the subject. *The Fishing Tackle Catalog* by Herbert Schaffner is a good place to start.

Chapter 3

© Hanson Carroll

THE ATLANTIC SALMON

Every year scores of fly anglers descend
upon the banks of the Miramichi River in
New Brunswick, Canada, eager to test their
skills (and their patience) against the
world's most well respected and highly

The adult Atlantic salmon has a blue-green back and silvery sides which are covered with black spots, sometimes X-shaped, lacking halos.

prized freshwater game fish, the Atlantic salmon. The Miramichi has long been considered one of the premier Atlantic salmon rivers in North America. While towns such as Chatham, Bartibog Bridge, Millerton, Renous, and Derby may not be well known to those outside New Brunswick, they are the regular yearly retreats of some of the world's greatest fly anglers.

On the Miramichi, the salmon are as plentiful as they are big. The first "brights" enter the river in early spring and make their way upstream until they reach their natal waters to spawn sometime in the fall. While the salmon fishing is good here, it is not generally a place for beginners or the easily distracted. In his book, *Fishing the Big Three*, Ted Williams, arguably the best pure hitter in the history of baseball and one of world's most successful sport fishermen, states that he makes between three hundred and four hundred casts for each salmon he catches. It is not unusual for even the most experienced angler to go for days without a strike. So why is the Atlantic salmon

considered such a prized catch, and why do anglers spend thousands of dollars on a fishing trip that may yield only a few fish? The answer is obvious to anyone who has ever seen a 20-pound (9-kg) Atlantic salmon leaping and thrashing at the end of his or her line.

The Atlantic salmon, or *Salmo salar*, is the most famous of all salmon species. A "bright" salmon —one fresh from the sea—has a blue-green back, silvery sides, and a white belly. Its head, body, and dorsal fin are covered with haloless black spots, which are sometimes

X-shaped. Just before spawning, the male develops a hooked lower jaw and takes on a pinkish hue.

Young Atlantic salmon, before entering the ocean, develop eight to eleven dark bars known as parr marks on their sides. These marks usually remain until just before the fish enters the ocean for the first time. At that time, the juvenile salmon take on a silvery hue and develop a forked tail fin.

Most salmon caught today weigh between 3 and 20 pounds (1.3 and 9 kg), although they can grow close to 100 pounds (45 kg). Catching a 20- to

© Ron Pittard/Windsor Publications, Inc.

25-pounder (9- to 11-kg) on a fly rod is considered quite an accomplishment, yet trophy-size 30-pounders (13.5-kg) are still taken on the Miramichi and its surrounding rivers from time to time. The largest Atlantic salmon are found in Norway; although, even there the size and numbers of these fish are quickly shrinking. The rod-and-reel record was set in Norway, when Henrik Hendrickson pulled in a 79-pound, 2-ounce (36-kg, 56-g) salmon in 1928. In 1902, Scottish poachers netted a 103-pounder (46-kg) at the mouth of the Devon River.

During the spawning season, Atlantic salmon are found migrating up rivers in Maine, Canada, the British Isles, Iceland, Greenland, Norway, Sweden, Finland, France, and Spain. At one time in North America, this noble fish was present as far south as the Connecticut River; however, the steady encroachment of civilization has all but wiped out salmon fishery in the United States and has drastically reduced populations in Canada. The dumping of chemical waste and sewage into rivers, the acidification of the waters from air pollution, rising tempera-

tures from global warming, the building of dams on spawning rivers, and a strain from commercial over-fishing, netting, and poaching have all contributed to the near demise of the North American salmon fishery.

Over the past twenty-five years, Canadian and New England wildlife officials and environmental groups have taken great strides toward preserving the future of the salmon. Many salmon rivers that were on the verge of collapse are now again able to support returning fish populations, thanks to the installation of fish ladders over dams, and the enforcement of stiffer pollution regulations. In addition, North American hatcheries have engaged in extensive stocking programs in an attempt to repopulate salmon rivers and streams. Mature salmon are captured, and their eggs and milt are removed without harming the fish. The eggs are hatched and the young fry are raised in captivity, and then eventually released. Once in the wild, these stockers go through the normal salmon life cycle, and treat the release stream as their spawning waters.

While the salmon population in United States rivers has grown considerable over the past few years, the vast majority of Atlantic salmon fishing in North America is still done in Canada. Below is a salmon fishery on Campabello Island, British Columbia.

Atlantic salmon fishing has long been considered the domain of the aristocracy. Many of Canada's top salmon rivers are controlled by private clubs that limit fishing to members, and the exclusiveness of these clubs rivals that of the most restrictive country club. Access to some rivers that are open to the public can also be very expensive. An angler may pay up to one thousand dollars a week to fish a prime section of river. Combine these steep river fees with travel, lodging, food, and a guide, and you have quite an expensive fishing trip. In addition, salmon fishing is not the type of sport in which you can go out for a day or two, catch your limit, and go home satisfied. It takes a great deal of time and persistence to effectively fish for salmon. In general, a week-long salmon trip is considered a short outing.

Most average anglers cannot afford the time and money needed for a rewarding trip even if they can find a productive public salmon river. Over the past several years, however, the Canadian government has begun to wrest the control of the rivers away from the private angling clubs. By refusing to renew river leases, the Canadians have begun to open up more and more salmon rivers to the public, making salmon fishing more accessible to the everyday angler. The revitalization of Maine's salmon rivers has also helped the situation somewhat; however, most of these rivers are still not yet frequented by many out-of-state anglers.

All Atlantic salmon spawn in fall in the same rivers and streams in which they were born. The initial salmon runs, however, begin several months earlier in the spring, just after a heavy rain oxygenates the river and raises the water level. Those first salmon to enter the rivers are referred to as brights. They are

© Dick Poe/Visuals Unlimited

strong and powerful, have a silver luster with a pinkish tint, and are not yet laden with eggs and milk. These are the salmon most sought after by anglers. They are energetic, determined, and put up quite a fight once hooked. In addition, they are probably the best tasting of all salmon. The fish that enter the stream later in the season, on the other hand, are much more "ripe," meaning they contain more roe and milt. Because

of their ripeness, these salmon are less aggressive and are not quite as exciting to catch.

Most salmon remain in the ocean for several years before returning to spawn. Some, however, known as grilse, return after only one year. Because of their limited time at sea, grilse are much smaller than fully mature salmon, averaging between 3 and 6 pounds (1.3 and 2.7 kg). There are a few rivers, in Maine particularly,

that feature primarily grilse runs, although most have a combination of grilse and full-grown salmon.

As stated in Chapter One, many Atlantic salmon, unlike their Pacific cousins, survive the debilitating ordeal of spawning. They remain in their native streams throughout the winter and then feed voraciously in the spring, before heading back out to sea. These "black salmon," or "kelts," are very easy to take in the spring,

A fly fisherman unfurls a nice cast. In North America it is illegal to fish for Atlantic salmon using anything except fly equipment.

© Gay Bumgarner/Photo/Nats

because they eat almost anything. As a result, fishing for kelts is illegal everywhere except for New Brunswick, Canada. And even there, very few serious anglers fish for them because the practice is considered unsportsmanlike. If allowed to return to the ocean, kelts come back to the rivers the following summer in record sizes.

In North America, it is illegal to fish for Atlantic salmon with anything except fly tackle. Over the past century, a whole subsection of the fly tackle industry has developed specifically for salmon fishing. The traditional salmon rod was a cumbersome 12- to 15-foot (3.6- to 4.5-m) fly rod weighing as much as thirty ounces. While a few of these monster rods are still used in parts of Europe, they are antiquated for the most part. Today, the trend is toward shorter and lighter rods, not much longer than those used for trout fishing. Most anglers use either an 8½-foot (2.5-m) for normal fishing situations, or a 9- to 9½-foot (2.7- to 2.9-m) rod for casting long distances or into heavy winds. Whatever length rod you choose, it should have

Courtesy Orvis Company, Inc. (all)

Efforts by the U.S. Fish and Wildlife Service (opposite page) have helped to restock a few U.S. rivers with the once prolific Atlantic salmon. From top to bottom: Three classic salmon flies: Irresistible, Black Dose, and Hairy Mary.

a fairly strong backbone and at least moderate casting power.

The large salmon fly reel (around 3¼ inches [8 cm] diameter) is slightly larger than a trout fly reel and should be loaded with about 150 to 200 yards (135 to 180 m) of 30-pound (13-kg) test backing line for large fish, or 15- to 20-pound (7- to 9-kg) test backing for smaller fish. Weight-forward line is good for all-around fishing; however, if you plan to do a lot of dry-fly fishing, you may wish to use a double tapered line. Because salmon are not as wary as trout, the length of the leader is not quite as important. When the water is flowing high and strong, a 7½ foot (2.2 m) tapered leader with a 2x tippet is sufficient. When the water is low and clear, however, you should go to a 9½-foot (2.8-m) leader.

Just like trout anglers, salmon anglers argue incessantly over what types of flies work better in particular situations. It's likely that many a barroom brawl has been started over which fly takes more salmon on the Penobscot in May—the Thunder and Lighting or the Silver Cosseboom.

About the only thing most anglers can agree on, however, is that darker flies work better on bright days, and brighter flies work better on overcast days. And even that age-old axiom doesn't always hold true.

Naturally, for any type of salmon-fishing success you must plan your trip to coincide with the fish's spawning run. The optimum time to be on the river is just as the first fish enter fresh water. Talk to fishing authorities and continually check local salmon reports. The importance of research cannot be overemphasized, especially when you may be laying out thousands of dollars on a single fishing trip. While salmon are very predictable and sometimes begin their run within a few days of a particular date year after year, such unpredictable factors as weather, temperature, and water level and flow may affect exactly when they begin their trek upstream.

They usually congregate near the mouth of the river before their run and wait for a heavy rain to oxygenate the water and raise river levels. Only when conditions are perfect do they enter the river. Once the run begins, the salmon move quickly, covering several miles in a single day. As long as the river level remains high, the salmon move upstream during the day and rest in pools at night. If the water level drops drastically, however, they find a pool and stay there until a rain comes and brings the level back up again.

If you are not familiar with the particular salmon stream you are fishing, it is essential to hire a guide.

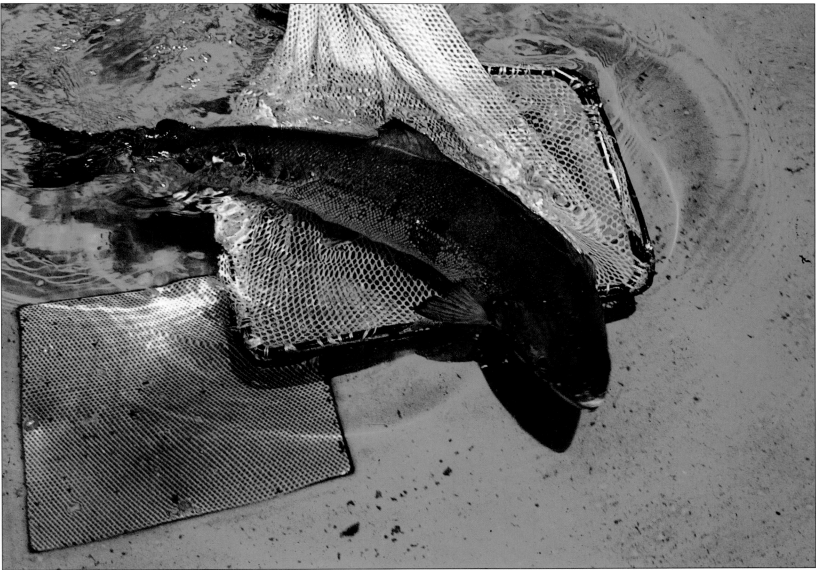

© U.S. Fish and Wildlife Service

In salmon fishing, unlike trout fishing, casting blindly rarely yields a salmon. You must locate the fish, cast to them, and try to annoy them into striking. An experienced salmon guide will know the migrating habits and holding spots of the salmon and be able to direct you to the river's hot spots.

Salmon generally hold in pools between 3 and 6 feet (.9 and 2 m) deep. Look for relatively shallow pools with a fairly swift current. Atlantics tend to avoid deep stagnant pools, although they may be found around the edges of a deep pool if no better holding spot is available. Like trout, salmon love to hang around structures and in shaded areas, especially in the middle of the day when the sun is hot. They usually rest next to undercut banks, under fallen trees, at the feet of dams and falls, under bridges, and around rocks and boulders. A particular favorite holding spot of the salmon is behind a large rock that splits a strong current. They also hold around the edges of pools where fast currents meet slower ones. When water levels are high, salmon hold over gravel bars and in shallow areas that are inaccessible when water levels are low.

An angler shows good form as he prepares to launch his fly upstream in hopes of catching a running Atlantic.

The spring run is the best time for salmon fishing. The salmon that run early in the season are much stronger and more active than those that run later. In addition, the fishing is usually good throughout the day in the spring. During the summer, salmon tend to move only in the morning and evening and are mostly inactive during mid-afternoon.

The fly fishing technique for salmon is different than it is for trout. Both salmon and trout anglers stand upstream from where the fish are holding; however, salmon anglers generally cast across and down-stream, whereas trout anglers may cast across and upstream. Most salmon are taken on wet flies fished just below the surface.

Position yourself about 50 feet (15 m) above the holding spot. While salmon are not as skittish as trout, you should still take care not to get too close or make too much noise in and around the river. Cast across and downstream at a forty-five degree angle and let the fly drift close to fish. The fly will pick up speed as the line tightens with the speed of the cur-

© Michael Kingsford/Envision

Even though salmon do not eat while on their spawning run, they can be coerced or teased into striking. The best way is to swing the fly broadside to the salmon and across its nose.

rent. The idea is to swing the fly broadside to the salmon and across its nose, thus angering it into striking. As the fly completes the swing downstream, lift the rod so that if a salmon strikes, you can quickly lower the tip and begin to play the fish. If at the end of the drift you don't get a strike, begin retrieving the fly with short yanks against the current.

During the late summer, when water levels are low, salmon often rise to take a dry fly. When hitting the surface, these normally heedless fish become a bit more wary, so it is necessary to use about a 10- to 12-foot (3- to 4-m) floating leader on your line. In addition, a double-tapered fly line helps with the soft, delicate casts necessary for dry fly fishing. Because the salmon are not eating, the choice of fly is not as important as it is when fishing for the wily brown trout. Any of the patterns mentioned earlier in this chapter should do. If you are not having success with one fly, then experiment with others until you find out what works. Cast the fly across and downstream and allow it to drift without any drag. Occasionally a

Because of their immense size, tireless fighting ability, and reluctance to strike, Atlantic salmon are considered the premier freshwater game fish in North America.

© U.S. Fish and Wildlife Service

© Shelly Rusten/Trout Unlimited

salmon comes up and meets the fly without striking. If this happens, keep casting; eventually the fish may hit.

Another angling method is to skim or skate a wet or dry fly across the surface. Here again, you cast across and downstream; however, with this technique you rapidly retrieve the fly so that it skips across the surface of the water, creating a wake. Attaching your fly with a riffling hitch will help the fly skim freely. To tie a riffling hitch, simply loop 2 or 3 half-hitches around the fly's head so that it hangs at a 45 degree angle from the leader.

The Atlantic salmon is one of the strongest fighters in the world of fish. If you feel a nibble, don't be too anxious to set the hook. The salmon may play with the fly a little while before actually striking. By yanking too soon you may pull the fly right out of the salmon's mouth. Salmon are big, strong fish and when they strike for real, you know it. Most times they set the hook in themselves without much effort from the angler. Once hooked the fish pitches a desperate battle to free itself. It will charge downstream and head for the near-

est white water or craggy protrusion. The key is to keep the salmon away from obstacles, while not putting too much strain on the line. At the beginning of its run, allow the fish to take as much line as it wants with moderate drag. If you try to reel it in too soon, you will snap the tippet and lose the fish. Because salmon are so strong, it is impossible to play the fish by holding the line in your hand, as you would with trout. Instead, you must play it directly from the reel. This is why it is important to have a good strong salmon reel when going after big fish.

© Hanson Carroll/FPG International

Once hooked, the Atlantic salmon will make dramatic, water-churning leaps. A typical salmon may jump three or four times before it finally gives up.

Part of what makes the Atlantic salmon such an exciting fish to catch are its high acrobatic leaps from the water. The fish will charge full tilt and suddenly burst through the surface of the water, head and tail flailing. A determined salmon may perform this heart-stopping spectacle three or four times in a single run before it finally gets free or gives up. Perhaps more than anything else it is the salmon's water-churning leaps that make it the most venerated freshwater fish in the world.

With increased restrictions on polluters, extensive stocking programs, and the opening up of Canadian salmon rivers, the outlook for Atlantic salmon anglers is brighter today than it has been in the past forty years. While Maine currently boasts the only remaining salmon rivers in the United States, fish and game officials are making continued efforts to repopulate rivers farther south in New England. If these rivers are made viable once more, and if stocking programs take hold, the outlook for the prestigious Atlantic salmon may become brighter still.

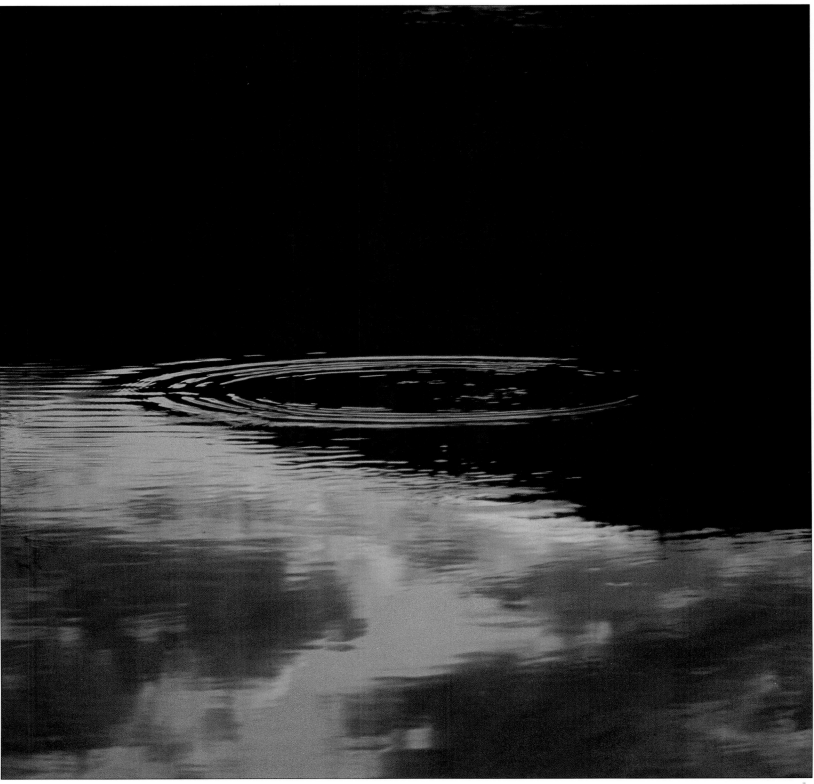

Chapter 4

© Ken Graham

LANDLOCKED SALMON

For anglers across New England, the spring break-up of the ice on their local lakes means one thing: salmon fishing. Scores of anglers brace themselves against the bone-chilling cold, and go out on the

A landlocked salmon is simply an Atlantic salmon that is trapped in fresh water and has lost its migratory instinct. The male landlocked (above) *is generally plumper and more colorful than the female* (below).

lakes with fly or spinning gear in hand. There, they cast from the banks or troll the shallow coastlines in hopes of hooking one of these hard-fighting fish. Though not quite as large or esteemed as their cousins, the Atlantic salmon, landlocked salmon are nonetheless exciting fish to catch. If caught in shallow water, they will thrash, run hard, and leap at the end of your line. It takes no small amount of skill to reel in one of these fighting fish, which is why landlocked salmon fishing has become extremely popular over the past several years.

The landlocked salmon, otherwise known as the Sebago salmon, Sebago trout, Schoodic salmon, lake salmon, or ouananiche, is simply an Atlantic salmon that is trapped in fresh water and has lost its migratory instinct. Instead of traveling out to the ocean, landlockeds survive in the lakes and tributary streams of Canada, Maine, New York, Vermont, and New Hampshire. It is believed that these fish have completely lost the instinct to travel to sea. In tagging experiments, landlocked salmon were placed in streams in areas where they would have easy access to the ocean. Instead of traveling to sea, they located a local lake and established a landlocked population there. Although they aren't literally landlocked, these fish prefer life in fresh water to a home in the ocean.

The landlocked's general appearance is similar to that of its saltwater counterpart. It has the same blue-

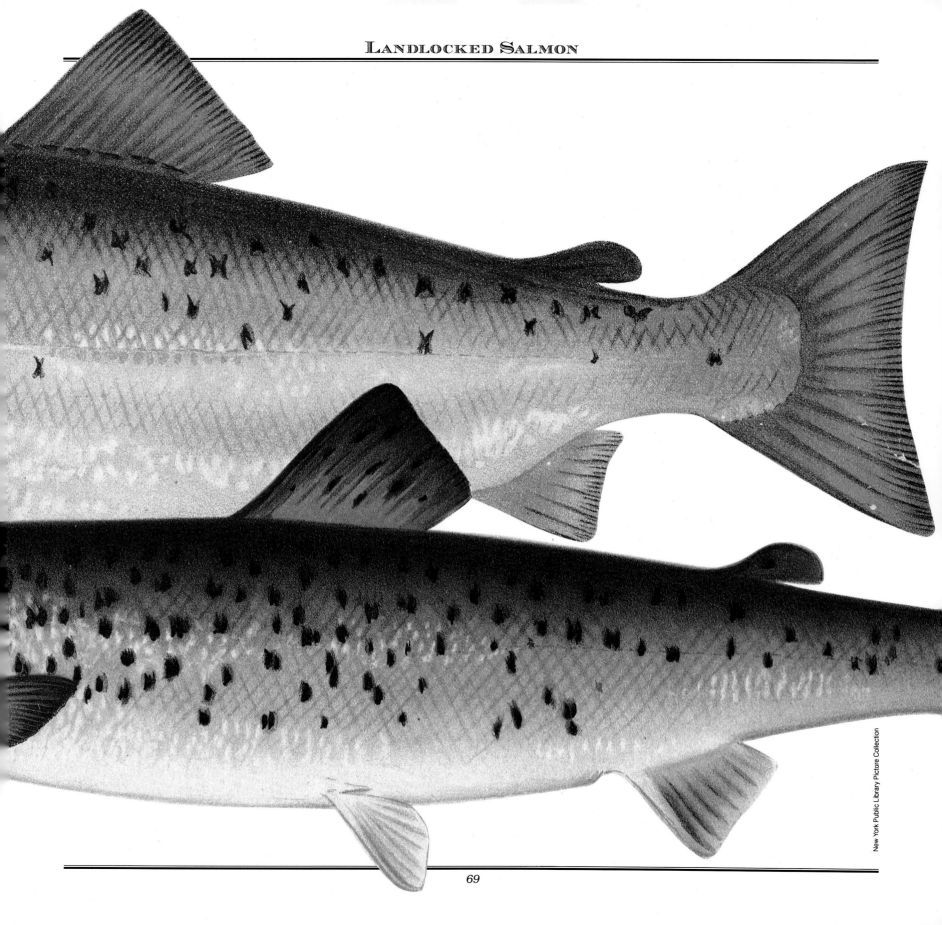

North American Landlocked Salmon Lakes

Maine	Big Lake, Dobis Lake, Eagle Lake, Grand Lake, Green Lake, Lake Chesuncook, Moosehead Lake, Mooselookmeguntic Lake, Pleasant Lake, Pococumas Lake, Sebago Lake, Spednic Lake, and Square Lake
New Hampshire	Big Dan Hole Pond, Big Squam Lake, Bow Lake, Lake Winnipesaukee, Merrymeeting Lake, Newfound Lake, Ossipee Lake, Pleasant Lake, Silver Lake, and Sunapee Lake
Vermont	Big Averill Lake, Caspian Lake, Crystal Lake, Dunmore Lake, East Long Pond, Echo Lake, Harvey's Lake, Little Averill Lake, Maidstone Lake, Seymour Lake, and Willoughby Lake
New York	Finger Lakes, Lake George, and Schroon Lake
Canada	There is good landlocked fishing in hundreds of lakes in Labrador, New Brunswick, Newfoundland, Nova Scotia, Ontario, and Quebec.

The popularity of landlocked salmon fishing has grown immensely over the past several years. There are now hundreds of lakes in Canada and the northeast United States with substantial landlocked populations.

green back and silvery sides with a pinkish tint; however, it lacks some of the Atlantic's markings and physical characteristics. The landlocked salmon does not usually have the distinctive double-X black spots of the Atlantic. In addition, its eyes are smaller and its fins shorter. The most obvious difference between the two fish is their size. Whereas a full-grown Atlantic salmon may weigh anywhere from 10 to 70 pounds (4.5 to 32 kg), the landlocked usually range between 3 and 7 pounds (1.3 and 3 kg). The rod and reel record is a 22½-pounder (10-kg) caught by Edward Blakely on August 1, 1907, in Sebago Lake, Maine; however, today a 10- to 12-pounder (4.5- to 5.4-kg) is considered a trophy fish.

These fish thrive in deep, cold North American lakes that contain large populations of smelt, their primary food. The most populous lakes are in Maine, including Eagle Lake, Moose-head Lake, Spednic Lake, and Sebago Lake, where the landlocked was originally identified. Over the past few decades, the fish has been introduced to the lakes and rivers of Argentina,

© William Moriarty/Envision

Fishing for landlocked salmon is much more accessible than fishing for Atlantic salmon. It is much less expensive and there are no tackle requirements; anglers can use spinning, bait-casting, or fly equipment.

where it has thrived. Today, some of the largest landlocked salmon in the world can be found in Argentina.

Whereas fishing for the Atlantic salmon is largely a pastime for the extremely wealthy, landlocked fishing is geared more toward the everyday angler. There are no exorbitant river fees to pay, and the lakes are not controlled by private angling clubs. In most locations, you will need access to a boat, and you may want to hire a guide when fishing strange waters. These expenses, however, are tiny when compared with the thousands of dollars you may spend on an outing for Atlantic salmon.

Another factor that makes fishing for landlocked salmon more accessible to the average angler is that there are no strict tackle requirements. Because the Atlantic salmon is considered a threatened fish, anglers may only fish for them with fly tackle. With landlocked salmon, on the other hand, the angler may use a variety of fly, trolling, spinning, and bait-casting gear. Even though all of this tackle is allowed, most anglers still opt for fly gear when going after landlockeds.

© Alan L. Detrick

Fly rods can be used both for casting and shallow-water trolling, and they provide most anglers with much more excitement and satisfaction in fishing. A 7½- to 9-foot (2.2- to 2.7-m) light- or medium-weight fly rod is good for nearly all salmon-fishing situations. The rod should carry a fairly large salmon reel loaded with 100 to 150 yards (90 to 135 m) of backing line. If you are casting streamers, use a weight-forward line for optimum casting distance and accuracy. If you are

fishing dry flies, use a double-tapered fly line for a more delicate approach.

The best time of year for catching landlocked salmon is in the early spring, just after the ice breaks up, usually in April in southern Maine and New York, and in May in northern Maine and Canada. The season usually lasts anywhere from two to six weeks, depending on the weather. As long as the water temperature stays between 40 and 45°F (4 and 7°C) the fishing should be good.

Spring is the time of year when large schools of smelt enter the lake's tributary streams to spawn, and the salmon usually follow. Instead of actually entering the tributary streams, however, the landlockeds will gather around the mouths of the streams and in the shallow water along the shore waiting for schools of smelt to cross their paths. They love to hold along rocky shorelines, drop-offs, and ledges that lead directly into deep water. As with the lake trout, the larger salmon sit in the deeper sections of a reef or shoal, and the smaller ones are scattered throughout. A favorite congregating spot for salmon is a bar or shoal that extends out into the lake and is surrounded by deep-water drop-offs.

Landlocked salmon love to feed in rough water. They usually stay in the choppiest sections of the lake, where the waves tend to pile up. The best

salmon fishing usually takes place on windy, drizzly, raw, cold days when the water is rough. On these days they tend to swim closer to the surface, and they feed voraciously. As a general rule, the more uncomfortable a day it is for the angler, the better the fishing will be. On calm, sunny days, salmon tend to stay closer to the bottom and eat less. If the sky is clear and the water

smooth, you will most likely have better luck fishing in the early morning or evening.

Trolling from a small boat with a fly rod is the most popular method for catching landlockeds in the spring, when they are in shallow water. Load your fly rod with medium sinking line to help get your streamer or bucktail deep enough. There is a wide variety of salmon and trout streamer flies that work well for trolling. A few good patterns to have on hand include Black Ghost, Silver Doctor, Black-nosed Dace, Mickey Finn, Edson Light, Barnes Special, and Dark Tiger. Use brighter colored streamers on cloudy days and in murky water, and use more drably colored streamers on clear, sunny days. Streamer sizes 2 to 6 will suffice for most situations.

Most boats have at least two or three rod holders on their stern. Increase your chances by trolling a line in each rod holder. Landlocked salmon are not overly boat-shy—in fact, they are sometimes attracted to the wake of the boat—so you can troll anywhere from 40 to 80 feet (12 to 24

© Ken Graham

While most anglers fish for landlocked from a boat, others prefer to cast from shore or to wade when the fish are in shallow water in the spring.

m) from the stern without scaring them. If you are using a few lines, stagger the trolling distances and depths until you determine where the fish are hitting. A speed of about four miles per hour is a good rate to start; however, you should experiment with different speeds until you find out what works. Fish in different lakes never behave quite the same. If you know where a lake's hot spots are, cover them thoroughly. As mentioned previously, if you are unfamiliar with the fishing waters, hire a guide to help you, or at the very least ask the advice of local anglers. When the water is choppy and the fish are eating, they will practically jump onto your line. If you are fishing calm water, troll at a slightly faster speed and add a little action to the streamer by raising and lowering your rod tip.

Casting for landlockeds from the shore is even more enjoyable than trolling for them. Here again, a streamer or bucktail fly is your best bet. Work the mouths of tributary streams and along jagged, craggy shorelines. Also, look for schools of smelt. Anyplace where there are

© Alan L. Detrick

Courtesy Orvis Company, Inc. (all)

From top to bottom: *Green Highlander, White Wulff, and Royal Wulff.* It is good to have a wide variety of flies and lures on any fishing trip.

smelt, hungry salmon are sure to be. Cast to the spot where you think the fish are holding and allow the fly to sink for a few minutes. Then begin to retrieve the fly with short, jerky motions. Do not be in too much of a hurry to retrieve your line. The salmon may look at your fly for a while before striking. Also, if you feel a slight hit, don't immediately try to set your hook. Salmon are not as selective as trout, and they usually hook themselves. By overreacting and trying to set the hook too soon, you may yank the fly right out of the fish's mouth.

Many times in late summer and early fall, the salmon are surface-feeding on a multitude of insects, so you are likely to have better luck fishing with a dry fly. The best times of day for dry fly fishing are in the morning and evening, when the fish tend to feed on insects. Depending on what the fish are eating, a variety of dry flies in sizes 8 to 14 should work. A few good flies include Light Cahill, Quill Gordon, March Brown, Black Gnat, White Wulff (or any of the Wulff series), Red Fox, and Adams.

While fly tackle is still the most popular equipment for landlocked fishing, more and more anglers are turning to spinning gear with either lures or bait, for both trolling and casting from shore. A medium-weight spinning rod and reel filled with 6- to 10-pound- (3- to 5-kg-) test line suffice for most casting and trolling situations. (For deep-water trolling, you need slightly different equipment.) The most popular lures for salmon are the Sidewinder, the Mooselook

Wobbler, and the Daredevle. Gold, silver, or fluorescent colored spoons also work very well, as do plugs such as Rapala and Rebel.

As with most types of fishing, natural baits are probably best for catching salmon. Live smelt—the landlocked's favorite food—seem to work best. When hooked by its lips or just under the dorsal fin, the live smelt swims and flutters freely at the end of the line, attracting many strikes from unknowing salmon. Alewives, minnows, and even the occasional nightcrawler also land salmon regularly.

When trolling shallow waters with lures, spoons, or plugs, you usually need little if any extra weight on your rig. If you're having trouble getting the lure deep enough, add one or two split-shot sinkers to the leader about 15 to 20 inches (37 to 50 cm) above the lure. Many anglers like to use a light-keel sinker when fishing with live smelt. This rig prevents the line from twisting and makes for a more natural-looking presentation.

Once hooked in shallow water, the landlocked salmon puts up a very

dramatic fight. Few freshwater game fish are as exciting to land. It runs hard and fast, stripping line off your reel as fast as your drag allows. Although not as skilled a fighter as the brown trout or the steelhead, the landlocked salmon is nonetheless very powerful. It will dart from side to side, shake on the end of the line, and most likely leap several times before tiring and rolling over. When fishing

with fly tackle, it is necessary to play the fish directly from the reel. If you attempt to play it with the line in your hand, as you would a trout, you are likely to lose the fish.

As summer rolls in and the smelt run ends, landlocked salmon abandon the increasingly warm, shallow water for the cool depths of the lake. During this time of year, they are much harder to locate and catch, and

once hooked, do not put up nearly as dramatic a fight. Yet, with the proper equipment and the right knowledge, you can enjoy good salmon fishing throughout the summer.

When the surface water is warm, salmon mostly stay in the thermocline layer of the lake. This is the portion of the lake where the water is rich in oxygen and the temperature stays at around 50°F (10°C). The

A group of anglers heads out for some early morning fishing. Following page: A fly fisherman hurls a beauty of a cast as his angling partner looks on.

thermocline varies from day to day and is at different depths at different portions of the lake. Depending on the time of year, the weather, the size of the lake, and the prevailing currents, the thermocline may be anywhere from fifty to two hundred feet (15 to 60 m) below the surface.

Deep-water trolling is the only effective method of catching salmon when they stay at this depth. For trolling, you need a medium to heavy, 6½- to 7-foot (1.8- to 2-m) freshwater or light saltwater rod loaded with 300 to 400 feet (90 to 120 m) of 15- to 20-pound (7- to 9-kg) test wire or lead-core line. The deeper the water you are trolling, the heavier pound test line you need.

The most effective lures for deep-water trolling are large 4- to 6-inch (10- to 18-cm) spoons or natural baits such as alewives, smelt, or yellow perch. It is also good to add one or more attractor spinners, or "cowbells," to your rig to gain even more attention.

Over the past few decades, more and more anglers are turning to downriggers for deep-water trolling. Using a downrigger allows the angler to employ much lighter tackle, which makes for more exciting fishing. A downrigger consists of a short arm attached to the back of the boat, loaded with wire line and cannonball weight. An angler simply attaches his or her fishing line to the downrigger with a clip. The rig is then lowered to the desired depth. Once a fish is hooked, the clip releases the cannonball, and the angler plays the fish with his or her lightweight tackle.

Locating salmon during the summer is difficult at best. Even with the expertise of a guide, it is still necessary to use a temperature probe and a depth finder to find the fish. Look for underwater ridges and jagged shoals that fall right at the thermocline. Also keep an eye out for schools of smelt. Even with a temperature probe, it may be necessary to experiment trolling at different depths until you find out where the fish are. Always start trolling deep and then gradually try shallower depths.

As fall rolls around, the water cools and landlockeds gradually move back to shallow water and begin actively feeding in preparation for

© Alan L. Detrick

their late fall spawning run. Whereas Atlantic salmon move from the ocean to their natal rivers to spawn, landlocked salmon move from the lakes to the tributary streams. They begin congregating around the mouths of the streams in September. Once heavy rain sets in and raises the water level in the streams, the salmon begin making their way to the spawning waters. During this time, fly fishing with long, hairy streamers is probably your best bet. Use the same angling methods you would for Atlantic salmon during their spawning run.

While the Atlantic salmon has had to wage a constant battle for survival over the past several decades, the landlocked salmon has thrived with relative ease. Pollution, damming, and overfishing is less widespread in the lakes and streams where land-lockeds live. In addition, aggressive stocking programs have helped maintain landlocked salmon populations. Nonetheless, the problems of water pollution and acid rain are beginning to reach into even the most isolated and pristine areas. Unless mankind is careful, even this relatively stable salmon fishery may eventually be threatened.

Chapter 5

STEELHEAD

In the winter, just after the December rains, thousands of silver and blue streaks can be seen darting up the Skykomish, Umpqua, Columbia, Trinity, Bella Coola, and thousands of other cold, fast-flowing

SALMON.   SALMON TROUT.

© Francis & Donna Caldwell

rivers of the Pacific Northwest. These dogged fish are hell-bent to reach their native spawning grounds. They leap over obstacles, traverse white-water rapids, and dodge hungry predators with a singular goal in mind: to reproduce. Along the banks of the northwest's icy yet scenic rivers, union-suited anglers of all walks of life try their hands at catching one

of the strongest fish in North America: the steelhead.

Each winter, thousands of these mighty fish desperately fight their way from the Pacific Ocean upstream to their original birthplace. Here they spawn. They will never see the product of their efforts, because, like the Atlantic salmon, they only pause long enough after spawning to

regain their strength before heading back out to sea.

By the middle of April, the tiny steelhead fry begin pushing their way out of the gravel. They remain in fresh water, eating and growing until they are large enough and strong enough to work their way downstream and into the Pacific Ocean. Once at sea, they join the Pacific

salmon in a long, circular oceanic migration, which takes them north to the Bering Sea, south into the deep waters of the Pacific, and then back to the ocean waters near their home stream. They may make this migration several times during the two-plus years they remain in salt water. Then, suddenly, an internal alarm clock goes off, telling the steelhead to return home, to the freshwater place of their birth.

Often referred to as the Atlantic salmon of the west, the steelhead (*Salmo gairdneri*) is not really a salmon at all, but an oceangoing strain of rainbow trout. However, because it often runs with the Pacific salmon, has very similar habits to the Atlantic salmon, and requires the same tackle and angling techniques needed to catch all freshwater salmon, it is included in this volume on salmon angling. In fact, the steelhead is the favorite quarry of western anglers who are unable to travel east to fish for the much revered Atlantic.

While in fresh water, the steelhead retains the same colorful markings as the rainbow. Its back is a metallic

© David E. Rowley/Envision

© Ron Pittard/Windsor Publications, Inc. (both)

blue or green, which shades into a more silvery green on its sides. The fish is dotted with dark spots all along the top, sides, head, and dorsal and caudal fins. Its belly is usually a silvery white. As with the rainbow, the most spectacular freshwater marking is the wide band of crimson or pink running along the lateral line of the fish from gills to tail. While this marking is present on the freshwater steelhead, it is not quite as brilliant or intense as on the rainbow trout; however, the dots and slash of crimson become more pronounced in males during the spawning season.

After going to sea, the steelhead quickly loses its coloring and becomes bigger, longer, and more streamlined than the rainbow. While in the ocean, this fish has a steel blue or greenish back, silvery sides, and dark spots on its back and tail. The steelhead gets its name from its coloring as well as its extremely strong skull, which, according to fishing lore, forced net fishermen to administer several strong blows from a club in order to kill the fish when brought on to a boat.

© Ron Spomer/Visuals Unlimited

In order to help preserve the species, many conservation-minded anglers practice catch-and-release fishing. Here an angler gently releases a prime specimen. Others, however, prefer to save their fish for the frying pan.

The largest and most exciting steelhead run takes place during the winter months; however, there are usually some of these fish running every month of the year, with the second largest run taking place during the summer. Winter steelhead are also the largest of the strain by far, sometimes reaching fifteen to twenty pounds (7 to 9 kg). Summer steelhead, on the other hand, usually weigh not more than 8 pounds (3.6 kg). The rod and reel record for steelhead is held by David White, who caught a 42-pound (10-kg) lunker on June 22, 1970, in Alaska.

The steelhead's natural range is from Alaska to northern California. The best steelhead fishing takes place in the cold, fast-flowing rivers of British Columbia, Washington, and Oregon. Once at sea these resourceful fish sometimes migrate for hundreds of miles. Steelhead schools often join or follow large schools of Chinook salmon on their oceanic journey.

In a tagging experiment in 1972, several hundred steelies were marked and released around the Aleutian Islands. Two years later, a few of them

were caught in the rivers of Washington State.

The steelhead is probably the most popular freshwater game fish among experienced West Coast anglers. In the East, steelhead fishing is virtually nonexistent. Many of the stocked rainbows in the east do make it to the ocean, but they do not carry the

strong migratory and spawning instincts of the western steelhead. There are a few steelhead stocking operations in the Great Lakes area, but natural reproduction has not been very successful.

Much of the steelie's popularity comes from its large size and extremely strong fighting ability.

There is always little doubt when a steelie strikes your line. It hits your fly or lure hard and fast, and then follows with a relentless, rod-bending fight. Steelies of all sizes make long, powerful runs, taking your line downstream through swift-running water, around rocks and other obstructions, and often down into

The Smith River in California (right) *is one of the many good steelhead rivers in the west.*

deep pools. Sometimes they run for 150 feet (45 m) or more while viciously tugging and shaking their heads back and forth trying to free themselves. Steelhead are extremely adept at snagging and breaking an angler's line on sharp rocks and fallen trees. Even the most experienced anglers consider it a good day when they land half of the steelies they hook.

The most exhilarating aspect of the steelhead's run is its spectacular, arched-back leap. Like the Atlantic salmon, an extremely feisty steelie may breech four or five times in a single run. It will swim full tilt at the end of your line and then hurdle completely out of the water, head and tail flapping, in a desperate attempt to free itself. And then, almost without losing a beat, the steelie will splash back down and continue its run with a swift stroke of its powerful tail. While a 4-pound (2-kg) brown jumping at the end of your line is thrilling enough, it just doesn't compare to the excitement of a 9-pound (4-kg) steelie thrashing 2 or 3 feet (.9 m) in the air.

© Frank S. Balthis/Nature's Design

Steelhead Rivers

British Columbia	Fraser, Kispiox, Cowichan, Skeena, Cooper, Sustut, Vedder, Thompson, Bella Coola, Babine, and Dean
California	Gaulala, Trinity, Sacramento, American, Russian, Feather, Smith, Yuba, Klamath, and Matole
Oregon	Columbia, Wilson, Sandy, Alsea, Deschutes, Coquille, Siletz, Umpqua, Rogue, Siuslaw, and Big Nestucca
Washington	Duckabush, Toutle, Kalama, Willapa, Stillaguamish, Nooksack, Snoqualmie, Bogachiel, Washougal, Naselle, Wind, Queets, Quinault, Rogue, Doeswallips, Wenatchee, Green, Puyallup, Lewis, Cowlitz, Skagit, Chehalis, Skykomish, and Nisqually

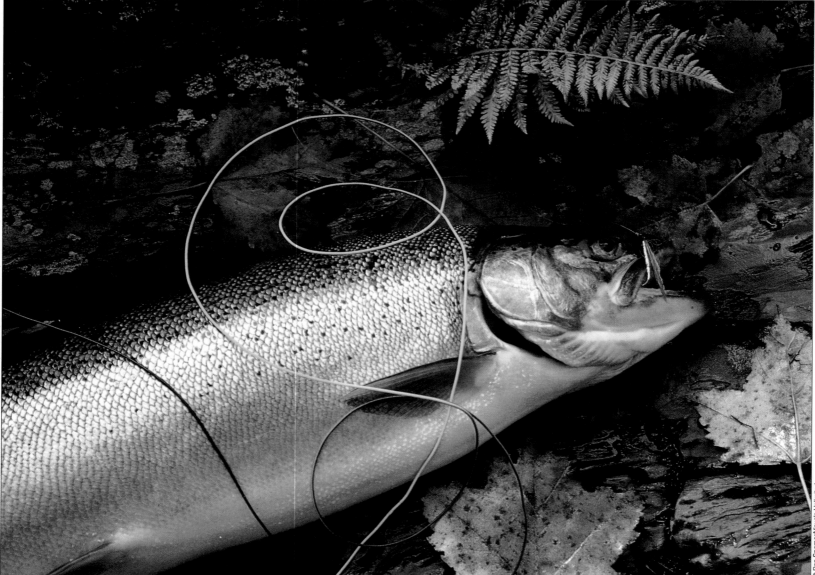

As with any type of fishing, the first and most important step in catching steelhead is locating them. This may prove to be a challenge, as steelhead runs may vary from river to river and from year to year. Steelhead do not adhere to a timetable quite as strictly as do Pacific and Atlantic salmon. Most rivers have one major run in the winter and one in the summer; how-

ever, even this is just a rough guideline. The bulk of the run may occur during different months from year to year, depending on weather, currents, and water levels. There are many rivers in Washington and British Columbia that have more-or-less continuous runs throughout the year, with slightly larger runs in the winter and summer.

Research is an essential part of any steelhead-fishing trip. Contact local fish and game authorities and area fishing stores to find out when the best runs take place and what to expect from local fishing conditions. On longer rivers, the runs are usually spread throughout the season. Different sections of the river are more productive at different times as the

© Ron Spomer/Visuals Unlimited

A 6½- to 8½-foot (1.9- to 2.5-m) rod with a medium-sized reel loaded with 9- to 15-pound (5- to 7-kg) test line is a very popular outfit with the average steelie angler...

fish move upstream. If you are lucky enough to live near a steelhead river, make several trips simply to observe the fish. Find out when they feed, where their holding spots are, and how long the run lasts. The more you know about the fish you are going for, the better your chances of success.

Just before an outing, always check weather reports around a potential river. A prolonged rain or sudden storm may cloud the water and put fishing at a standstill for days or even weeks. Most steelhead will not feed when the water level rises quickly and becomes murky. Once the river clears, however, fishing will again become productive. If there has been a recent rainstorm, concentrate most of your fishing in the headwaters and small tributary streams. These areas of the river will clear much faster than the lower portions.

Steelhead are particularly sensitive to sudden temperature shifts, especially during the winter run. If the water temperature drops off rapidly, the fish will become inactive and do very little feeding. For optimum fishing, the water should be

above 40°F (7°C). On particularly cold days, do most of your fishing during the mid-afternoon, after the sun warms up the water a bit. On the other hand, a sudden heat wave during the summer run may also make the steelie lethargic and unwilling to strike. During the summer heat, the best time to fish is early morning or evening.

As steelhead move upstream to their spawning grounds, they tend to lie in several different holding spots along the way. These "rest stops" are usually protected from the strongest currents. Steelhead hold around the edges of fast waters or at the heads or tails of riffles and runs. Like other trout and the Atlantic salmon, steelhead are structure lovers. They will

rest around boulders, sunken tree trunks, carved-out banks, rock ledges, under bridges, and at the bases of dams. Also, look for them around the edges of large pools; they will very seldom go in the deepest section of a pool.

Once you find a well-frequented steelie rest stop, you will be in for some electrifying fishing. Anglers use a wide variety of outfits when fishing for steelies—everything from ultralight fly rods, to heavy surf-fishing rods. (Unlike the Atlantic salmon, it is legal to fish for steelies with spinning gear.) For years, the outfit of choice was a 6½- to 8½-foot (2- to 2.5-m) spinning rod with a medium-size spinning reel fitted with 9- to 15-pound (4- to 7-kg) test line. Silver, gold, and brass spoons in various weights and sizes usually work well in the steelie's fast-moving rivers. Some of the most successful lures are imitation salmon-egg clusters such as the Oakie Drifter and the Spin and Glo, as well as wobblers such as the Lil Jasper and Fat Max, and cherry bombers such as Luhr Jensen Fireplug and Prism Glo.

...however, more and more anglers are enjoying the extra challenge of catching beauties such as this steelie with a fly outfit.

© Ron Spomer/Visuals Unlimited

When fishing steelhead with a lure, be sure to drift-fish the lure along the bottom fast enough so that you can actually feel the action of the spinner blade. Drift the lure as close to obstacles and the river floor as possible without snagging your rig on the bottom. With practice, you will become more familiar with the feel of your rod and the action of your lure, and snags will become less prevalent. If you never snag your line, however, you are probably not fishing deep enough. Steelies are bottom feeders, and will not strike too close to the surface. If snagging becomes a major problem, you may want to replace the treble hook on your lure with a single hook. Also, be sure to have several lures with your tackle. You are sure to lose at least a few on bottom.

As you fish a certain section of river, study it well. Make mental note of where obstacles are, where the currents flow, where the pools form, and, most importantly, where the fish are holding. The longer you fish the same hole, the better you will become at guiding your lure in and around pools and obstacles, taking

A netted steelhead trout gets pulled from the river (right), while a proud angler displays his trophy-sized catch.

© Ron Spomer/Visuals Unlimited

it right to the fish's mouth. If it is an extremely productive hole, try to commit as much of it to memory as you can. You may even consider writing down a few notes about it before you leave. That way, if you return to that hole on a day when the water is deeper or less clear, you will still have a good idea where the obstacles are and where the fish are holding.

Many anglers rely on natural bait for catching steelies. The most successful of the natural baits is a handmade egg cluster or a fresh roe sack. Egg clusters can be bought in a jar at most fishing stores, or you can make your own using fresh roe. To do this you place the eggs in the center of a small square of maline netting. Gather the corners of the netting together and tie them with a piece of thin thread. Other good natural baits include crawfish tails, night crawlers, and minnows (where legal). In many rivers, fishing with minnows is illegal, because careless anglers have introduced foreign minnow species, and thus tipped the river's delicate natural balance. Many of these minnows feed on the eggs and fry of trout

and salmon species, reducing the populations of valuable game fish.

The most traditional bait-fishing rig is still the most effective and easiest to handle. Tie a three-way swivel to the end of your line. To the top eyelet of the swivel tie two to three feet (60 to 90 cm) of 8-pound- (3.6-kg-) test monofilament leader with a

hook at the end. To the lower eyelet, tie a four- to six-inch (10- to 13-cm) piece of 4-pound- (1.8-kg-) test (or lower) leader with a sinker attached. It is best to use a pencil sinker, because it will be less likely to snag. If it does snag, however, you will be able to break it off easily because of the weakness of the sinker leader.

Simply give a short, hard tug on the line and the sinker should break away. You should always have plenty of pencil sinkers in your tackle box when fishing for steelies.

The method for fishing with a bait is slightly different than for fishing with a lure. Position yourself directly downstream from where the fish are holding. Cast the bait 30 to 40 feet (9 to 12 m) above the hole and let the bait sink nearly to the bottom. Be extremely careful with your cast when fishing with this method. If you come up short on a cast, you will startle the fish and ruin your chances. Inexperienced anglers who are not confident in their casting ability should consider fishing from upstream and letting the bait drift down past them. As the bait begins to roll with the current, keep the rod tip low and take in just enough line to control the bait. If you have too much slack, you will lose the fish when it strikes. When the method is working properly, you will be able to feel the

© Alan L. Detrick

While many people do fish for steelhead using spinning and baitcasting gear, others believe that the true sport comes in catching them on a fly rod.

sinker bouncing along the bottom. You should respond with a sharp tug at even the slightest indication of a strike.

Fishing for steelhead with lures and natural baits is still extremely popular, however, the real sport comes in catching these mighty fish on a fly rod. The most popular fly outfit for steelhead is an 8- to 9½-foot (2.4- to 3-m) graphite or bamboo fly rod loaded with slow-sinking or medium-sinking fly line. Because steelhead are primarily bottom feeders, wet flies and streamers are most effective. You can also take steelhead with virtually any salmon pattern and with many trout patterns. Any knowledgeable steelhead angler will have at least a few of these patterns on hand: Royal Coachman, Silver Ant, Thor, Gray Hackle, Skykomish, Cummings, Umpqua, Silver Demons, Van Luven, Queen Bess, Harger's Orange, Fire Fly, Burlap, and Kalama Special.

The most common method for fishing steelhead with a fly differs somewhat from Atlantic salmon fishing. Instead of casting across and downstream, the steelhead angler

Here, an angler admires a keeper he pulled from the Pescadero Creek in California.

should use the same technique as with other trout. Cast across and slightly upstream at about a 45-degree angle. Then, let the fly sink and drift downstream into the prospective hole.

Many steelhead anglers use a somewhat more complicated variation of the Atlantic salmon method. With this technique you cast across and slightly downstream. As soon as the fly touches the water, begin to dip and raise the rod tip once every five seconds with a slow and rhythmic movement. As you do this, strip in about a handful of line at a time. You should strip in a total of about 2 to 3 feet (60 to 90 cm) of line during the entire drift. Let the fly drift downstream until it begins to work its way back across stream, and continue the rhythmic motion. Once it gets about three quarters of the way across stream, begin a slow retrieve.

It is important that your fly sink to the correct depth. Soak your fly well before casting. Some anglers even go so far as to dip their flies in mud to make them sink quickly. If your fly still isn't sinking properly, consider

The calm before the strike. An angler anxiously waits along the banks of the Pescadero for a hit from a steelhead.

changing to a quicker-sinking line and leader, or add a small split-shot sinker to your line.

When fighting a big steelhead with a fly rod, don't attempt to strip in line with your hand. You will have much better success playing the fish with the reel. Steelies will break loose with even the slightest kink or misplay. Let the steelie take out line and tire itself; however, try to keep it from running through obstacles or into fast-running water. Landing a steelhead takes a great deal of skill and patience. Once hooked they will immediately head downstream for white water. While you do want to try to guide the fish away from white water and sharp obstacles, if you attempt to reel it in too soon, you will most assuredly lose it.

At certain times during the late summer and early fall, steelhead feed on insects hatching on the surface, making dry fly an effective mode of attack. When dry fly fishing, use a ten- to twelve-foot (3- to 4-m) long floating leader with a fine tippet that allows the fly to drift naturally. (When fishing with wet flies or streamers you

Steelhead are among the most exciting and challenging game fish in North America. They are powerful fish that don't give up without a fight.

won't need quite as long a leader [6 to 10 feet (1.8 to 3 m)], and the leader should sink.) Casting is all-important to the success of a dry-fly angler. The cast must be accurate and gentle, so that the fly lands on the water without creating an unnatural disturbance. As the fly drifts slowly with the current, keep the line taut enough so that you can react in case of a strike, but not so tight as to create a drag and alter the drift. A few good dry-fly patterns for steelies include Grey Wulff, Black Wulff, Steelhead Bee, and Surface Stonefly.

Steelhead offer some of the most challenging and exciting sport fishing in North America. Steelhead angling is much more accessible to the everyday angler than Atlantic salmon fishing. There are many productive steelhead rivers that don't command the prohibitive river fees of the Atlantic salmon rivers.

This is not to imply that fishing for steelies is easy. Your first few steelhead trips may be extremely frustrating. You will, most likely, lose fish after fish, and deposit a great deal of tackle on the river floor. Every out-

ing, however, will be a learning experience as you get to know the ins and outs of your equipment and the determined fighting characteristics of the steelhead. Even the most seasoned anglers are continually challenged by the fighting ability of this

powerful fish. Once you experience the thrill of a 10-pound (4- kg) steelie jumping at the end of your line, you will quickly understand why countless anglers eagerly look forward to the bone-numbing conditions of the winter steelhead run.

Chapter 6

© Ruth Fairall

THE PACIFIC SALMON

Dog, blueback, Kokanee, king, silver, humpback, chum, sockeye, spring, Tyee, blackmouth, cherry, Chinook, coho, pink, and more…there seem to be almost as many names for the Pacific salmon as there

The many types of Pacific salmon support both a huge commercial and recreational fishing industry.

are rivers in the Pacific Northwest. In fact, almost every riparian local in the northwestern United States and western Canada has at least a few regional names for various species of Pacific salmon. Perhaps this is because no other region in North America has been quite so influenced by the salmon. When the glaciers that ripped through the Pacific Northwest began to diminish more than ten thousand years ago, the salmon were among the first life forms to repopulate the then-desolate area. They swam up the rivers from the ocean and helped replenish vast amounts of nutrients in the depleted land. Many biologists believe their role in replenishing the land explains why the Pacific salmon, unlike the Atlantic, die immediately after spawning.

Many centuries later, countless Native American cultures were completely reliant upon the salmon for survival. They used the salmon's pink, tender flesh for food, and their oil for fuel. They even worshiped the salmon as a spiritual icon. When the first white settlers entered the area,

they too grew dependent on the salmon as a means of sustenance and later developed the salmon cannery as their primary industry.

Many animal species still rely on the salmon as a major source of food. Seals, otters, porpoises, and killer whales are just a few of the oceanic life forms that ravenously feed on these fish. During the spawning runs, bears line the banks of the rivers in hopes of snagging a fresh meal. Trout, squawfish, and ducks all feed on the salmon eggs and young fry. After the spawning is over and the Pacific salmon die, bald eagles, buzzards, and other scavengers feed on the lifeless fish. And those salmon that are not devoured decay and return important nutrients to the rivers and soil.

Despite all of the local names given to this important fish, biologists have determined that there are just five North American species of Pacific

salmon: the Chinook (*Oncorhynchus tshawytscha*); the coho (*Oncorhynchus kisutch*); the sockeye (*Oncorhynchus nerka*); the chum (*Oncorhynchus keta*); and the pink (*Oncorhynchus gorbuscha*). (There is a sixth species, the cherry salmon, which is found only in Asia and will not be covered in this book.) While anglers do fish for all five of these salmon species to some extent, most of their efforts are aimed at catching Chinook and coho, the two most desirable species. The Chinook salmon and the coho salmon will be discussed in detail later in the chapter, after brief summaries of the other three species.

SOCKEYE SALMON

While the sockeye, or blueback, salmon is not particularly sought after by the game angler, it is the primary fish caught by the commercial salmon industry. Thousands upon thousands of these tasty fish are hauled in by oceangoing commercial trawlers and shipped across the United States and Canada. There are a few anglers who fish for sockeye,

After their long arduous journey upstream to spawn, the adult Pacific salmon die. Their carcasses then become food for scavengers such as bald eagles, bears, and buzzards.

© Alissa Crandall

© Gerry Ellis/Ellis Wildlife Collection

There is a flash of red as a group of running salmon charge upstream to their spawning waters.

but most are taken by anglers fishing for steelhead or other salmon.

While in the ocean, the sockeye has a bluish green back, silvery sides, and fine speckling. In fresh water, however, it takes on a brilliant coloration, especially around spawning time. The male's body turns bright red and its head a contrasting pale green. The coloring of the female is usually less intense, characterized by green and yellow splotches. This is a relatively small member of the Pacific salmon family, usually weighing no more than eight pounds (4 kg). The sockeye naturally ranges from the Bering Strait to the Sacramento River in California.

One strain of sockeye, known as the Kokanee, has lost the instinct to migrate to the ocean. This land-locked fish is a bit smaller than the oceangoing sockeye (weighing between 2 and 3 pounds [.9 and 1.3 kg]) and lives primarily in cool lakes and their tributary streams. The Kokanee has developed a moderate following among freshwater anglers in the western and midwestern United States and in southern Canada, where these fish have been introduced. A few Kokanee have been stocked in eastern lakes, but populations have yet to take hold.

CHUM SALMON

The chum, or dog salmon, is a close relative of the sockeye. Like the sockeye, it has a bluish green back and silvery sides when in salt water. After it returns to fresh water to spawn, the chum develops reddish bars and large pale blotches on its sides. Its oceanic range is from the Arctic Ocean to the Pacific coast of southern California. Inland it can be found in coastal streams as far south as the Sacramento River.

Even though it can grow to upwards of 30 pounds (13.5 kg), the chum is probably the least popular of all Pacific salmon, because it is easy to catch, does not put up a fight, and doesn't taste very good.

PINK SALMON

Another of the smaller Pacific salmon, the pink, or humpback, salmon has a maximum weight of about 10 pounds (4.5 kg), with the

There are several different types of Pacific salmon that inhabit North America. Below: From left to right are examples of Chum, Pink, and a young Coho salmon. Opposite page is an adult Coho.

average weight at between 4 and 6 pounds (2 and 3 kg). Like the sockeye, most pinks are taken by commercial trawlers. They do not readily take bait or a lure when in the ocean, and they never travel very far upstream before spawning. They are a popular game fish in the Washington State's Puget Sound, where they are caught primarily with bait or lures. Pink salmon are identifiable by the hump the male develops on its back just before spawning time.

COHO SALMON

The coho, or silver salmon, along with its close relative the Chinook, is one of the most popular game fish in the Pacific Northwest. It also supports a large commercial fishery in the area. While not quite as large as the Chinook, a big coho can nonetheless tip the scales at about 25 to 30 pounds (11 to 13 kg), although most weigh between 10 and 20 pounds (4.5 and 9 kg). The coho's upper body is bluish green and fades to silver on the sides and white on the belly. It also has irregular black spots on its back and upper caudal fin. These impressive salmon can be found in the ocean from the Bering Strait to Baja, California, and in coastal streams as far south as Mon-

terey, California. Since the 1960s, there has been a hugely successful stocking program in the Great Lakes and their surrounding rivers. In fact, the coho salmon found in the Great Lakes tend to be much larger than those in the Northwest. In the Great Lakes, 15- to 20-pounders (7- to 9-kg) are quite common, while on the West Coast, a 12-pounder (5-kg) is considered a collector's item. (More on the Great Lakes Salmon Fishery later in the chapter.)

Juvenile coho stay in fresh water for about a year and then migrate out to sea where they stay for three to four years before reaching maturity.

© Chris Huss/Ellis Wildlife Collection (all)

© David Csepp/Ellis Wildlife Collection

Mature coho leave the sea during the early summer and spawn in the late fall or early winter. Some may remain in fresh water for up to eight months before spawning.

The vast majority of coho fishing in the west is done in the ocean from charter and private boats. Unlike most other salmon species, coho are homebodies that never migrate very far from their spawning river. They usually feed close to the surface just off the mouths of their river, making them a favorite of fly and light-tackle anglers.

When trolling for coho with light tackle, look for schools of swarming bait fish, such as anchovies or herring. Usually a concentration of coho will be nearby. Coho tend to travel in large schools, so once you see a few fish, chances are there are hundreds more. Coho are extremely skittish when feeding on the top, so it is best to troll around the edges of a feeding school, at a slow speed so as not to scare the majority of the fish into deeper water.

For trolling cohos, most fly anglers use a 9½- to 10-foot (2.8- to 3-m), medium-weight fly rod, and a large salmon reel loaded with 250 yards (75 m) of 10-pound (4.5-kg) test back-

While a lot of Pacific salmon fishing is done in the ocean, many anglers go for them in fresh water during their spawning runs.

ing line. Cohos are not picky eaters, so any long-bodied salmon streamer will do. Medium-weight spinning tackle is also good for trolling coho. Here again, the spinning reel should be loaded with at least 250 yards (225 m) of 10-pound (5-kg) test. Small saltwater spoons or fresh bait such as herring or anchovies work best.

Instead of trolling, many light-tackle aficionados prefer to cast for cohos from a small boat. To do this, simply let anchor, or drift your boat about 30 yards (27 m) from a feeding school and make casts toward the middle of the school. Once your fly, bait, or lure sinks a bit, begin retrieving it with short, jerky motions. Once you hook a surface feeding coho on light tackle, you will be in for a good fight. A 10- or 15-pounder (4.5- or 7-kg) will fight with every last bit of ocean-bred strength it has. Let it take line after it hits. If you try to reel it in too quickly, it will most certainly break free. When it begins to tire, bring the fish in by pulling back on the rod and then reeling in as you bring the rod tip forward. Again, play it carefully until you know it's yours.

© Don Johnston/Photo/Nats

© Francis & Donna Caldwell

Trolling or casting for surface-feeding cohos with light tackle is by far the most exciting and challenging way to catch them in the ocean; however, the vast majority of coho and Chinook are taken in deep water on heavy trolling tackle or with the use of downriggers. Large party boats armed with depth finders carry scores of anglers, and often pull in hundreds of salmon. While this is not the most challenging fishing in the world, it is enjoyable nonetheless, and very few fish taste as good as the oceangoing coho.

CHINOOK SALMON

The Chinook, or king salmon, is the largest of all Pacific salmon species, rivaling the Atlantic in both size and beauty. Mammoth Chinooks, weighing more than 125 pounds (56 kg) have been caught by commercial trawlers; however, most weigh between 15 and 35 pounds (7 and 16 kg). The rod-and-reel record is a 93-pound (42-kg) monster caught off the coast of Washington State. The coloring of the Chinook is very similar to that of the coho. It has a greenish-blue-to-black back, silvery sides, and a white belly. Aside from being larger than the coho, the Chinook is also a much more muscular and broad fish. The Chinook has a range from the Bering Strait to southern California, and it spawns in rivers as far south as the Sacramento. Like the coho, the Chinook has been successfully introduced into the Great Lakes region where an extremely large fishery is maintained.

The Chinook is the true nomad of Pacific salmon. After spending about a year in fresh water, young Chinooks head out to sea where they begin their

© Ken Graham

Salmon will sometimes travel hundreds of miles upstream to their spawning grounds. Unlike Atlantic salmon, Pacific salmon never survive to spawn a second time. Also known as the king salmon, the Chinook (near left) is the largest of all Pacific salmon species.

five-year, two-thousand-mile odyssey. While at sea, these ravenous eaters grow at the rate of 4 to 6 pounds (1.8 to 2.7 kg) a year, feeding voraciously on anchovies, crustaceans, squid, and their favorite food, herring.

In the spring and early summer, the offshore salmon tend to stay in very deep water. As the season rolls on they start to come a little closer to the surface, and peak fishing usually occurs around late August or early September. The most popular method for catching both Chinook and coho is with a downrigger. A downrigger is simply a short arm attached to the back of the boat that holds a cannonball weight and wire line. This device allows anglers to get their bait or lure deep into the water, while still using relatively light tackle. The angler simply attaches the fishing line to the downrigger line with a clip. The whole rig can then be lowered to the desired depth. Once a fish strikes, the line is automatically released, allowing the angler to fight the fish on medium-weight tackle.

Herring and anchovies seem to be the best bait for deep-water trolling,

You would be smiling too if you caught two such beautiful Chinook. These fish were caught on the Kenai River in Alaska.

although smelt, mackerel, and squid also work well.

Mooching is another popular method of offshore salmon angling. To do this, you need about an eight-or nine-foot (2- to 3-m) saltwater rod with a lot of backbone, loaded with about 250 yards (225 m) of 25- to 30-pound (11- to 15-kg) test. Herring or anchovies are also the best bait here. The basic technique of mooching is very similar to jigging. Drift the boat over a school of salmon located with a depth finder, then lower the rig about 40 or 50 feet (12 to 15 m). Start with your rod tip near the surface of the water, and then begin raising it in long sweeps above your head and then lowering it back down to water surface. This motion will cause the bait to dart and dance in the water, attracting many hungry fish.

Both Chinook and coho salmon are relatively easy to catch, once they are located in the ocean. They are easiest to catch during the prime season, when affordable charter and party boats constantly leave port from San Francisco, Seattle, and other West Coast cities. The skippers

A school of Chinook parr make their way from their birth place to the ocean, where they will grow for several years before returning to spawn.

© Chris Huss/Ellis Wildlife Collection

Today, coho salmon of the Great Lakes tend to be several pounds larger than western cohos, and while the Chinook have not quite reached poundage of their western cousins, they are sizable fish. While most West Coast salmon fishing is done in salt water (a few are taken in fresh water during the spawning runs), the Great Lakes fishery offers midwestern anglers the unique opportunity to fish for Pacific salmon in nearby freshwater venues. Many anglers maintain that the salmon fishing in the Great Lakes is better, more challenging, and more exciting than the ocean fishing in the Pacific.

Lake Michigan boasts the best salmon fishing of all of the Great Lakes. Because this was the first lake where the salmon established natural populations, the fish tend to be bigger than those in other Great Lakes. Salmon between 15 and 20 pounds (7 and 9 kg) are regularly taken by anglers in Lake Michigan. In fact, the rod-and-reel record for coho (30 pounds [13 kg]) was set on the Little Manistee River, just off Lake Michigan.

of these boats know their business well, and even the most unskilled anglers fishing from these boats are almost guaranteed to catch at least one fish.

THE GREAT LAKES SALMON FISHERY

In the mid-1960s, fish and game officials began ambitious plans to transplant the coho and Chinook salmon into the Great Lakes. First, coho were stocked in Lake Michigan, and then a year later, Chinook were introduced to the same lake. Soon the stocking program spread to the rest of the Great Lakes. As optimistic as midwestern anglers and fishery officials may have been, none could have predicted just how very successful this program would turn out to be. The fish thrived in the cool waters of these northern lakes and their tributary streams and, by the mid-1970s, salmon populations were well established.

Stocking programs of Chinook and coho have succeeded beyond most fishery officials' expectations. Here several anglers cast their lines as the sun rises over Lake Superior.

© Bob Firth/Firth PhotoBank

The Great Lakes coho and Chinook follow a predictable yearly migratory pattern, like salmon everywhere. In Lake Michigan, the fishing season begins after "ice out" in April. During this time of year, most of the salmon are in the southern part of the lake, off the shores of Indiana and Illinois. Most early fishing is done close to shore, either by shallow trolling from a boat, or by surf casting from the shoreline. Many salmon can be taken around the mouths of rivers where they wait for small bait fish on their spawning run.

As the water begins to warm up in mid-May and early June, the fish migrate north and begin to move into deeper waters. By mid-August most of the salmon are in the center of the lake. The summer migration of the salmon generally follows the level of the thermocline, the cool, well-oxygenated layer of water most suitable to fish (between 45 and 55°F [7 and 12°C]). Finally, by October and November, the salmon reach the northern part of the lake and begin their spawning runs in the tributary streams and rivers.

The bait or the catch? An angler decides whether or not to release this tiny fish, or simply use it as bait.

The majority of Great Lakes salmon fishing is done in early summer by trolling from boats. Any successful trolling trip requires three essential ingredients: a depth finder, to find schools of salmon or bait fish; a temperature probe, to locate the thermocline; and either a guide or an experienced angler familiar with the hot spots of the lake.

Downrigger trolling is method of choice on the Great Lakes and the best tackle for this is a 7- to 9-foot (2- to 2.7-m) medium spinning or bait-casting rod and a medium to heavy trolling or spinning reel. The best rods for this type of fishing have a limber tip for proper play of the fish. Because the salmon may be as deep as 100 or 150 feet (30 or 45 m), it is best to have between 200 and 250 yards (180 and 225 m) of 15- to 20-pound (7- to 9-kg) test mono line. Some particularly ambitious anglers enjoy using lightweight, or even ultralight rods with their downriggers when the fish aren't in particularly deep water; however most anglers need a little more backbone in their rods, for pulling in these large fish.

A pair of coho salmon show off their spawning colors. The more colorful of the two is the male.

If you don't have the luxury of a downrigger, then you need much heavier tackle to reach the proper depths. Wire or lead-core lines testing between 20 and 30 pounds (9 and 13 kg) and heavy saltwater-type trolling rods and reels are essential. In addition, you need an 8- to 15-ounce (22- to 42-gm) trolling weight and a six-foot (1.8-m) 30- to 40-pound (13- to 18-kg) test mono leader. Trolling with this type of equipment, while very effective, is not nearly as exciting as landing a big fish on lighter-weight tackle.

Most anglers use a variety of crankbaits and lures to attract salmon. Among the more popular types on the Great Lakes are Rapala, Rebel, Headhunter, Tadpolly, Flatfish, Pike Minnow, and Redfin. In addition, natural baits such as herring and smelt also work well (although with smelt you may land more lake trout than salmon). One of the most effective rigs is a series of attractors, such as cowbells or flashers attached above the bait or lure. These attractors can gain the attention of the most finicky of salmon.

In the fall when the salmon begin their spawning run, they can be taken in the tributary rivers and streams or in the river inlets and shallows of the lake using fly equipment or light spinning gear. Mature fish caught early in the spawning run are the fiercest and best-tasting

Chinook and coho stocking programs in the Great Lakes have opened up salmon fishing to many anglers who may have otherwise never had the chance.

salmon the Great Lakes have to offer. The Great Lakes coho and Chinook do not feed when on their spawning runs, so they have to be agitated into striking. Large, gaudy flies and hairwigs similar to those used for Atlantic salmon seem to be the best for landing these fish. Unlike with Atlantic salmon, however, the angler is also allowed to use spinning gear and lures to catch these running Pacific transplants. Flashy metallic spoons and small plugs are the angler's best bet when using spinning gear.

The Great Lakes fishery has opened up the thrill of landing large salmon to a wide variety of anglers. Unlike fly fishing for Atlantic salmon, angling for transplanted cohos and Chinooks is both affordable and highly accessible. In days when salmon populations in general are threatened by such factors as pollution, commercial overfishing, and the building of dams and other man-made obstacles, the Great Lakes stocking program has taken effective and positive steps toward preserving this noble fish.

© Hanson Carroll

Bibliography and Recommended Reading

Bergman, Ray, edited by Edward C. Janes, *Fishing with Ray Bergman.* New York: Alfred A. Knopf, Inc., 1976.

Buckland, John, *The Simon & Schuster Pocket Guide to Trout and Salmon Flies.* New York: Fireside Books/Simon & Schuster, 1987.

Evanoff, Vlad, *The Freshwater Fisherman's Bible.* New York: Doubleday, 1980.

Flick, Art, *Art Flick's Streamside Guide to Naturals and Their Imitations.* New York: Nick Lyons Books.

Ginrich, Arnold, *The Well-Tempered Angler.* New York: Plume, 1987.

Hackle, Sparse Grey, *Fishless Days, Angling Nights.* New York: Fireside Books/Simon & Schuster, 1988.

Haig-Brown, Roderick L., *A River Never Sleeps.* New York: Crown Publishers, 1974.

The Hunting and Fishing Library, *The Compleat Freshwater Fisherman.* New York: Prentice-Hall Press, 1987.

Kaufmann, Randall, *Fly Tyer's Nymph Manual.* Western Fisherman's Press, 1986.

LaFontaine, Gary, *Caddisflies.* New York: Nick Lyons Books, 1981.

Leiser, Eric, *The Complete Book of Fly Patterns.* New York: Knopf, 1977.

Lilly, Bud and Paul Schullery, *Bud Lilly's Guide to Western Fly-Fishing.* New York: Nick Lyons Books, 1987.

Lyons, Nick, *Bright Rivers*. New York: Fireside Books/Simon & Schuster, 1977.

Lyons, Nick, *The Seasonable Angler*. New York: Fireside Books/Simon & Schuster, 1988.

Maclean, Norman, *A River Runs Through It*. Chicago: University of Chicago Press, 1983.

Marinaro, Vince, *In the Ring of the Rise*. New York: Nick Lyons Books, 1976.

Rogers, Keith A., *Freshwater Fishing*. Champagne, IL: Leisure Press, 1987.

Rosenthal, Mike, *North America's Freshwater Fishing Book*. New York: Scribner, 1984.

Schaffner, Herbert, *The Fishing Tackle Catalog: A Sourcebook for The Well-Equipped Angler*. New York: Gallery Books, 1989.

Schullery, Paul, *American Fly Fishing: A History*. New York: Nick Lyons Books, 1987.

Schweibert, Ernest, *Nymphs*. Winchester Press, 1973 (out of print).

Soucie, Gary, *Soucie's Fishing Databook: Essential Facts for Better Fresh & Saltwater Fishing*. New York: Winchester Press, 1985.

Swainbank, Todd and Eric Seidler, *Taking Freshwater Game Fish*. Woodstock, VT: The Countryman, Press, 1984.

Wulff, Lee, *The Atlantic Salmon*. Nick Lyons Books, New York, 1986.

INDEX